S. Hrg. 113–625

THE EBOLA EPIDEMIC: THE KEYS TO SUCCESS FOR THE INTERNATIONAL RESPONSE

HEARING

BEFORE THE

SUBCOMMITTEE ON AFRICAN AFFAIRS

OF THE

COMMITTEE ON FOREIGN RELATIONS
UNITED STATES SENATE

ONE HUNDRED THIRTEENTH CONGRESS

SECOND SESSION

DECEMBER 10, 2014

Printed for the use of the Committee on Foreign Relations

Available via the World Wide Web: http://www.gpo.gov/fdsys/

U.S. GOVERNMENT PUBLISHING OFFICE

94–193 PDF   WASHINGTON : 2015

For sale by the Superintendent of Documents, U.S. Government Publishing Office
Internet: bookstore.gpo.gov   Phone: toll free (866) 512–1800; DC area (202) 512–1800
Fax: (202) 512–2104   Mail: Stop IDCC, Washington, DC 20402–0001

(II)

CONTENTS

ADDITIONAL MATERIAL SUBMITTED FOR THE RECORD

(III)

THE EBOLA EPIDEMIC: THE KEYS TO SUCCESS FOR THE INTERNATIONAL RESPONSE

WEDNESDAY, DECEMBER 10, 2014

U.S. SENATE,
SUBCOMMITTEE ON AFRICAN AFFAIRS,
COMMITTEE ON FOREIGN RELATIONS,
Washington, DC.

The subcommittee met, pursuant to notice, at 10:35 a.m., in room SD–419, Dirksen Senate Office Building, Hon. Christopher Coons (chairman of the subcommittee) presiding.

Present: Senators Coons, Durbin, Shaheen, and Flake.

Also Present: Senators Markey and Murphy.

OPENING STATEMENT OF HON. CHRISTOPHER A. COONS, U.S. SENATOR FROM DELAWARE

Senator COONS. Good morning. This meeting of the Senate Foreign Relations Subcommittee on African Affairs will come to order.

We are going to do things a little differently than usual today because of a rare honor for this subcommittee. Joining us from the Liberian capital of Monrovia today via video conference will be President Ellen Johnson Sirleaf, who will share with us her observations on the Ebola outbreak and its impact on her country.

President Sirleaf is an extraordinary individual who has already once pulled her country back from the brink of collapse following Liberia's long and destructive civil war. Her certainty of purpose, coupled with a vigorous commitment to reconciliation and economic recovery, make her the single best person to be leading Liberia through this very difficult time.

President Sirleaf has shown extraordinary leadership for her country in this time of crisis and continues to be an example for all in public service. Winner of the Nobel Peace Prize and Africa's first elected female head of state, President Sirleaf is an individual of exemplary character, fortitude, and compassion for her people.

I would also like to take a moment to recognize Mr. Jeremiah Sulunteh, the Republic of Liberia's Ambassador to the United States, who, like Madam President, has played a key role as a long-time servant to the Republic.

It is an honor and a privilege to have you with us today.

President Sirleaf has also volunteered to answer a few questions from members of the subcommittee following her remarks. It is a rare honor and an extraordinary opportunity to be joined by video conference by a sitting head of state, one for which my colleagues and I are grateful.

Madam President.

STATEMENT OF HER EXCELLENCY ELLEN JOHNSON SIRLEAF, PRESIDENT, REPUBLIC OF LIBERIA, MONROVIA

President SIRLEAF. Good morning. Thank you for inviting me to offer remarks at this hearing.

I would like to start by extending warm and profound gratitude on behalf of the people and Government of Liberia to the American people, the U.S. Government, the many American institutions and faith-based organizations for the leadership your country has taken by joining us on the frontline of this battle to turn the tide against this unknown disease that has threatened our very way of life.

My colleagues from Guinea and Sierra Leone, also victims of this disease, join me in these sentiments.

Allow me to recognize also the extraordinary work of U.S. Ambassador Deborah Malac and the Embassy team.

Chairman Coons and Ranking Member Flake, I would like to express my heartfelt thanks for the personal commitment demonstrated by you and other Members of Congress through your numerous phone calls and messages of support.

We express appreciation to President Obama for the bold steps, including the work of Dr. Tom Frieden, director of the Centers for Disease Control, and Rajiv Shah, the Administrator of USAID, in coming to our aid. It was the United States that awakened the world to the scope and magnitude of the Ebola disease's virulent spread in West Africa, that led to the extraordinary step to deploy the United States military to help Liberia. It was the leadership of the Obama administration, supported by Congress, that opened the space for the disease to stabilize in Liberia and encouraged the rest of the world to respond to this global crisis. It is a demonstration of leadership as important as the role to combat terrorism and other ills around the world.

We applaud the construction of Ebola Treatment Units by the DOD and the establishment of the field hospital to treat health care personnel as a significant and timely response to our predicament.

Today, our Armed Forces, which worked with the DOD, can boast of the capability to construct Treatment Units and other similar type of facilities. The Treatment Units send a powerful message to our people that Ebola is real, that it requires an overpowering response, and that the people of the United States stand by us. The units serve us well by ensuring that we can respond to continuing hotspots and possible recurrence.

The fact that they are not full is a strong sign of their success and shows that by working together with overwhelming force, we have begun to push back on this unknown killer disease.

Honorable Members of Congress, several of you may recall that on March 16, 2006, shortly after being elected President in Liberia's first post-conflict elections, I had the honor to address a joint meeting of the U.S. Congress and said that we will pay any price to lay the foundation for durable peace. In 2013, we celebrated the 10th year of peace that enabled us to achieve over 7 percent average annual economic growth, a 50-percent reduction in the infant mortality rate, 17 additional years in life expectancy, relief from a crippling external debt, and a restoration of economic and social infrastructure. Perhaps more importantly, we have established a free and democratic society, thus reversing the many decades of authoritarian rule.

This year incredibly changed everything. Like the rest of the world, we knew nothing about this disease. It sprung on us at the worst of times. Our subregion had just begun to recover from years of instability and commenced the process of regional integration. The three most affected countries have embarked on a path of democratic governance. As natural resource-rich countries, we were in the process of attracting investors, creating the conditions to accelerate growth with development. This has all been unimaginably reversed.

Today, we are fighting to keep people alive, facing a faceless but deadly enemy. As I speak to you, the Ebola virus has caused a serious disruption of Liberia's social, economic, and cultural fabric. It has destroyed many of our hard-fought development gains, wreaked havoc on our economy, exposed the weakness of our public health systems, interrupted our infrastructure development, closed schools, restrained travels, and shattered the lives of our people. The disease has subjected us to a stigma all over the world, creating a fear more destructive than Ebola itself.

With the support of partners like you, we have made progress in containing the virus. Our 13 emergency treatment units, with a total of 840 beds, have only 136 patients. Our 70 burial teams have buried 23 persons per day across the country, compared to hundreds months ago. We have seen a drop from around 100 new cases per day at the peak of the epidemic to only 10 confirmed new cases per day over the past week. Our six active laboratories have tested 60 samples a day but, on average, only find 8 new Ebola cases per day. The 4,000 contact tracers, which involve community workers, are following some 7,000 persons. Doctors, nurses, and other health care workers, some 174 of the over 3,000 who have died, are no longer at risk because quality treatment facilities are available to them. We are happy to say that 1,312 persons, including 345 children, many of them orphans, have walked away free from the disease.

Can I profoundly say I am excited about this progress? Yes, I am. But I also know that more has to be done, as we are now in the most critical stage of response. At 10 new cases a day, the crisis is now manageable, but experts tell us that traveling that last mile to zero new cases will be much more difficult because the disease has retreated and must now be chased down in every corner.

To illustrate this, consider the challenge of contact tracing. For each of the patients in the United States, there were around 40 contacts that needed to be quarantined and monitored. The challenge in Liberia is greater, with thousands more contacts, often in villages which take hours to reach through densely forested terrain. This is one of the many reasons why your continued support and our joint collaboration is so important. Moreover, full eradication will not be secured until the whole region is freed from Ebola, until there is prevention against future possible outbreak, until we develop a medicine both preventive and curative to conquer this deadly disease.

Yesterday, Liberia hosted a regional technical summit with Sierra Leone, Guinea, and Mali to share lessons and best practices.

The summit drove home the point that Ebola is not a Liberian issue or a West African issue. It is a global issue that we must all continue to confront. This is why continuing your assistance to the combined effort with our neighbors remains a priority. This is why the United States has been right to tackle it at the front line, here in West Africa. This is why Dr. Margaret Chan, Director General of WHO, was right when she noted that this is the greatest peace-time challenge the United Nations and its agencies have ever faced.

In Liberia and in Sierra Leone and in Guinea, we continue to live this challenge. As our response evolves, we ask that partners continue to support our efforts. This calls for strengthening community ownership and responsibility for awareness and immediate response action through the Community Care Centers that are being established with the support of USAID.

Here are a few statistics in this regard. Liberia has 218 medical doctors and 5,234 nurses to serve a 4.3 million population at 405 public and 253 private health facilities. This means we have 1 doctor for 100,000 people, compared with 4 for 100,000 in Sierra Leone, 10 for 100,000 in Guinea, and 245 for 100,000 in the United States. As we speak, there are more Liberian doctors and medical professionals in the United States than at home. Most of them left during the war, and we were in the process of trying to get them back home with incentives that measure up to their qualifications. This disease has upset that effort.

Clearly, we are far behind and can only sustain the progress and prevent a recurrence through better trained and better equipped health facilities, better diagnosis facilities for infectious diseases, better hospitals, better clinics. We have asked the 137 partners from some 26 countries who are with us in this fight to join us in this expanded effort.

Above all, Liberia must get back on the path to growth. My government is preparing a comprehensive plan for Liberia's post-Ebola economic recovery, accelerating our work in infrastructure, above all Roads to Health, electricity, and WATSAN operations. A major push in the agricultural sector, where most Liberians are employed, will enable us to generate jobs and restore livelihoods. The private sector will play a crucial role. In this regard, we commend the private sector organized under the Ebola Private Sector Mobilization Group with the efficacy of ECOWAS and the African Union for their support in making people and resources available to fight the disease. Their efforts will be even more critical in the building of post-Ebola economies, requiring from us commitment to create conducive conditions for private capital to succeed.

Liberia is extremely proud that we achieved the MCC Compact eligibility in 2012 by passing 10 out of the 20 indicators, including control of corruption. Liberia again passed eligibility in 2014 by passing 10 of the 20 indicators. Liberia has surpassed the MCC's Control of Corruption standard for seven straight years, one of the few developing countries to do so. An MCC grant would be a game changer for Liberia. It would facilitate our post-Ebola economic recovery and put our development momentum back on track, leading to substantial transformation of our economy.

I want to conclude by expressing our gratitude to you, the U.S. Congress, for the friendship and assistance, without which we would not have made the progress to date.

There remains a lot to do to ensure the resources are properly deployed by the many institutions to which it is directly allocated to ensure that there is full accountability to you and to all our partners, and to the Liberian people. Our resolve to meet the challenge that confronts us is strong and unrelenting. We will win this battle.

Once again, I want to thank you and the American people for the opportunity to be with you in this meeting today.

[The prepared statement of President Sirleaf follows:]

PREPARED STATEMENT OF HER EXCELLENCY ELLEN JOHNSON SIRLEAF

Chairman Coons, Ranking Member Flake, distinguished Members of the Senate Foreign Relations Subcommittee on African Affairs, Friends of Liberia, good morning. Thank you for inviting me to offer remarks at this hearing.

I would like to start by extending warm greetings and profound gratitude of the people and Government of Liberia to the American people, the U.S. Government, the many American institutions, and faith-based organizations for the leadership your country has taken by joining us on the front line of this battle to turn the tide against this unknown disease that has threatened our very way of life. My colleagues from Guinea and Sierra Leone, also victims of this disease, join me in these sentiments. Allow me to recognize also the extraordinary work of U.S. Ambassador Deborah Malac and the Embassy team.

Chairman Coons and Ranking Member Flake, I would like to express my heartfelt thanks for the personal commitment demonstrated by you and other Members of Congress through your numerous phone calls and messages of support.

We want to express appreciation to President Obama for the bold steps, including the work of Tom Frieden, Director of the Centers for Disease Control, and Rajiv Shah, the Administrator of USAID in coming to our aid. It was the U.S. administration that awakened the world to the scope and magnitude of the Ebola disease's virulent spread in West Africa; that took the extraordinary step to deploy the U.S. military to help Liberia. It was the leadership of the Obama administration supported by Congress that opened the space for the disease to stabilize in Liberia and encouraged the rest of the world to respond to this global crisis. It is a demonstration of leadership as important as the role to combat terrorism and other ills around the world.

We applaud the construction of Treatment Units by the DOD and the establishment of the field hospital to treat health care personnel as a significant and timely response to our predicament. Today, our Armed Forces which worked with the DOD can boast of the capability to construct treatment units and other similar type of facilities. The treatment units send a powerful message to our people that Ebola is real that it requires an overpowering response and that the people of the United States stand by us. The units serve us well by ensuring that we can respond to continuing hotspots and possible recurrence. The fact that they are not full is a strong sign of their success and shows that by working together with overwhelming force we have begun to push back on this killer disease.

Honorable Members of Congress: Several of you may recall that on March 16, 2006, shortly after being elected President in Liberia's first post-conflict elections, I had the honor to address a joint meeting of the U.S. Congress and said that we would pay any price to lay the foundation for durable peace. In 2013, we celebrated the 10th year of peace that enabled us to achieve over 7 percent average economic growth, a 50-percent reduction in the infant mortality rate; 17 additional years in life expectancy, relief from a crippling external debt, and a restoration of economic and social infrastructure. Perhaps more importantly we have established a free and democratic society thus reversing the many decades of authoritarian rule.

This year changed everything. As the rest of the world, we knew nothing about this disease. It sprung on us at the worst of times. Our subregion had just begun to recover from years of instability and commenced the process of regional integration. The three most affected countries had emerged from the days of instability and embarked on a path of democratic governance. As natural resource rich countries, we were in the process of attracting investors, creating the conditions to accelerate growth with development. This has all been reversed. Today, we are fighting to keep people alive, facing a faceless but deadly enemy.

As I speak to you, the Ebola virus has caused a serious disruption of Liberia's social, economic, and cultural fabric. It has destroyed many of our hard fought development gains, wreaked havoc on our economy, exposed the weakness of our public health systems, interrupted our infrastructure development, closed schools, restrained travel, and shattered the lives of our people. The disease has subjected us to a stigma all over the world, creating a fear more destructive than Ebola itself.

With the support of partners, we have made progress in containing the virus. Our 13 Emergency Treatment Units, with a total of 840 beds, has only 136 patients. Our 70 burial teams have buried 23 persons per day across the country compared to hundreds, months ago. We have seen a drop from around 100 new cases per day at the peak of the epidemic, to only 8 confirmed new cases per day over the past week. Our six active laboratories have tested 60 samples a day, but on average only find 8 new Ebola cases per day. The 4,000 contact tracers which increasingly involve community workers are following some 7,000 persons. Doctors, nurses, and other health care workers, some 174 of whom died, are no longer at risk because quality treatment facilities are available to them. We are happy to say that 1,312 persons including 345 children, many of them orphaned, have walked away free from the disease.

Am I excited about this progress? Yes, I am! But I also know that much more has to be done for we are now in the most critical stage of response.

At 10 new cases a day, the crisis is now manageable; but experts tell us that traveling that last mile to zero new cases will be much more difficult, because the disease has retreated and must now be chased down in every corner. To illustrate this, consider the challenge of contact tracing. For each of the patients in the U.S., there were around 40 contacts that needed to be quarantined and monitored. The challenge in Liberia is greater, with thousands more contacts, often in villages which take hours to reach through dense bush. This is one of the many reasons why continuing support your support and our joint work together is so important.

Moreover, full eradication will not be secured until the whole region is freed from Ebola; until there is prevention against future possible outbreak and until we develop a medicine, both preventive and curative to conquer this deadly disease. This is why securing our borders remains a priority requiring additional resources, as well as providing assistance to our neighbors. On yesterday, Liberia hosted a regional Technical summit with Sierra Leone, Guinea, and Mali to share lessons and best practices. The summit drove home the point that Ebola is not a Liberian issue or a West African issue. It is a global issue that we all must continue to confront. This is why the U.S. has been right to tackle it at the front line, here in West Africa. This is why Dr. Margaret Chan, Director General of WHO, was right when she noted that this is greatest peacetime challenge the United Nations and its agencies have ever faced." In Liberia, and our Mano River Union neighbors of Sierra Leone and Guinea, we continue to live this challenge.

As our response evolves we ask that partners continue to support our efforts. This calls for strengthening community ownership and responsibility for awareness and immediate response action, through the Community Care Centers that are being established with the support of USAID. Here are a few statistics in this regard. Liberia has 218 medical doctors and 5,234 nurses to serve 4.3 million population at 405 public and 253 private health facilities. This means we have 1 doctor for 100,000 people, compared with 4 per 100,000 in Sierra Leone, 10 per 100,000 in Guinea and 245 per 100,000 in the United States. As we speak, there are more Liberian doctors and medical professionals in the United States than at home. Most of them left during the war and we were in the process of trying to get them back home, with incentives that measure up to their qualifications. This disease has upset all of this effort.

Clearly we are far behind and can only sustain the progress and prevent a recurrence through better training and better equipped health facilities. We have asked the 137 partners from some 26 countries who are with us in this fight to join us in this expanded effort.

Above all, Liberia must get back on the path to growth. My government is preparing a comprehensive plan for Liberia's post-Ebola economic recovery, accelerating our work in infrastructure—above all Roads to Health, electricity and WATSAN operations. A major push in the agricultural sector, where most Liberians are employed, will enable us to generate jobs and restore livelihoods. The private sector will play a crucial role.

In this regard, we commend the private sector organized under the Ebola Private Sector Mobilization Group (EPSMG), with the advocacy of ECOWAS and the African Union for their support in making people and resources available to fight the disease. Their efforts will be even more critical in the building of post-Ebola economies requiring from us commitment to create conducive conditions for private capital to succeed.

Liberia is extremely proud that we achieved MCC compact eligibility in 2012 by passing 10 out of 20 indicators, including control of corruption. Liberia again passed eligibility in 2014 by passing 10 out of 20 indicators. Liberia has surpassed the MCC's control of corruption standard for 7 straight years, one of the few developing countries of the world to do so.

An MCC grant would be a game changer for Liberia. It would facilitate our post-Ebola economic recovery and put our development momentum back on track leading to substantial transformation of our economy.

I want to conclude by expressing our gratitude to you, the United States Congress, for the friendship and assistance, without which we would not have made the progress to date. There remains a lot to do—to ensure the resources are properly deployed by the many institutions to which it is directly allocated; to ensure that there is full accountability to you and all our partners and to the Liberian people. Our resolve to meet the challenge that confronts us is strong and unrelenting. We will win this battle. Once again, I want to thank you and the American people for the opportunity to address you today.

Senator COONS. Thank you, Madam President. Thank you for your remarks with us today, and thank you for the opportunity for several of our members to ask a few questions.

I might just begin with one question, and I think we might restrict ourselves to one question each, if we might.

I want to make sure, Madam President, that we are providing the right resources both to meet the emergency that you so correctly point out is not over and we need to remain engaged on as an international community, the pressing and current emergency of Ebola. But I also am wondering if we are providing the right resources to rebuild your public health infrastructure and to overcome what you referenced, a stigma that is in some ways a fear of Ebola that is greater than Ebola itself in terms of long-term challenges for your economic recovery.

Are we providing the right assistance, and are we helping you rebuild for the future in the right ways?

President SIRLEAF. The resources to contain the virus are for the moment adequate to do so, as the progress has shown. However, there is always the chance of reoccurrence, as the history has shown in other countries that have been affected by the disease. This is why we must now move from containment, from treatment to prevention, and to do that means we will need the resources to rebuild, to strengthen our health care facilities, our hospitals, our clinics, through training, through better equipment, through better facilities. That way we can ensure that there will not be a reoccurrence, or in the event of a recurrence we will have the means to control it and to prevent its spread, not only within our country but as it spreads across borders.

And that is why today we are working with our partners to get them to join us in this transition to prevention, working with our own people, our Community Care Workers, taking full responsibility by being trained to handle basic health care, particularly in our rural areas.

Senator COONS. Thank you, Madam President.

Senator Flake.

Senator FLAKE. Thank you, Madam President. Thank you for appearing here today. I wanted to thank you for what you have done to rally the international community to join the effort to, as you say, stop the epidemic in West Africa.

We are pleased to hear the progress that Liberia is making, and our concern that similar progress has not been made in Sierra Leone. You mentioned that you have come together with leaders in other countries and public health officials.

What are you doing to make sure that best practices are shared and that the progress that has been made in Liberia is replicated elsewhere? Can you give us some idea of what is going on there?

President SIRLEAF. The coordinator of the President's Advisory Ebola Committee is today on his way to start discussion that will put him in the position to become a general coordinator for the three countries, working with UNMEER, the U.N. coordinating agency that is based in Accra. At the meeting held yesterday, Liberia offered, and I had already obtained President Roman's agreement to that, to send some of those nurses and doctors that we have over to Sierra Leone, with the agreement, of course, to be able to join the Sierra Leone forces in trying to expand their own capacity to deal with the disease. We expect that we will be looking at the results of yesterday's meeting to see what else Liberia can do to be able to join Sierra Leone particularly because they seem to be right now the ones in most serious trouble.

But we will do everything that we can, share every capacity that we have, every resource we have, to be able to work with them so that they can get the same progress. Because, like I say, until the other two countries are free, Liberia cannot be truly free.

Senator COONS. Thank you, Madam President.

Senator Durbin.

Senator DURBIN. Madam President, thank you. Let me tell you that your statement about the number of doctors and medical professionals in Liberia is sobering and evidences a dramatic need for more medical resources in your country.

Our immigration bill that we considered 2 years ago would have allowed, for example, Liberians practicing medicine in the United States to go back to Liberia and West Africa and to help on an emergency basis without jeopardizing their immigration status in the United States, and I hope we can return and pass something of that nature very quickly next year.

But my specific question to you is this. The United States and President Obama are making substantial investments in West Africa to address Ebola. Many, many other countries are joining in that effort. I applaud all of their efforts.

What is being done in Liberia to make certain that the investments that are being made are part of a transition in Liberia to a stronger public health system? The investments in equipment, in laboratories, in training of health care workers? Is Liberia working with these nations to make sure that there is a long-term commitment to strengthening the public health system in your country?

President SIRLEAF. Congressman, first of all, I am so glad about the immigration law, and I wish it would be reintroduced and would pass to enable our Liberian doctors to come and work with us.

I am so pleased that with the support of the Clinton initiative we had before Ebola worked on and finalized a 10-year health system improvement plan. That plan has in it the training of thousands of health care workers that would be placed throughout the country, in all areas. It also has the upgrading of facilities by better equipment, better facilities.

So this is our plan. We are now discussing that plan with the partners who are here working with us on Ebola and engaging them to start the transition from working on Ebola to support for our health care system, because that is the most lasting way to contain Ebola and to contain similar diseases such as malaria, on which we have made substantial progress and which could be reversed if we do not have the infection control system through a better health care delivery system.

Senator DURBIN. Thank you.

Senator COONS. Thank you, Madam President.

Senator Shaheen.

Senator SHAHEEN. Thank you very much, President Sirleaf, for your willingness to join us today and for your resolute leadership to address the Ebola crisis that has threatened not only Liberia but Guinea, Sierra Leone and other countries in Africa.

As you know, one of the mandates of the U.N. mission for Ebola Emergency Response is to help work with the governments affected to reinforce the leadership of those countries, including Liberia, and I wonder if you could talk a little bit about how that part of the U.N. mission has been working and whether the cooperation is helpful, and are there other things that can be done to improve that cooperation.

President SIRLEAF. The support has been most helpful to us. The mission works with us as we plan our responses not only for Ebola but responses in all of our development initiatives. There could be more coordination because we do have many partners that join us in this, and what we are doing is trying to ensure that we set up the mechanism that will enable us to be able to continue to monitor the progress that is being made, to continue to revise plans and to upgrade them to meet extenuating circumstances.

So at this stage we are very pleased with the support of the mission, and when it comes to the USAID mission, I have to say that I cannot start saying so much for the Administrator, Rajiv Shah, who has just worked with us through all of this in so much, and has worked with so many of the other missions in the other countries that enable us to coordinate that, not only on a national basis but on a regional basis.

Senator SHAHEEN. Thank you.

Senator COONS. Thank you, Senators.

Madam President, thank you so much for your remarks to us today, thank you for your leadership, and thank you for the opportunity to continue to work in partnership as we invest in sustaining the recovery of your nation, lay the foundation for a strong public health system, and work tirelessly together to ensure that this outbreak of Ebola is brought to an end. Thank you very much.

President SIRLEAF. Chairman Coons, I thank you and all of you, the members of the subcommittee, for this opportunity, and thank you for the support that you continue to give to Liberia, not only in this fight but in our overall development effort.

May I stay and listen to some of it? [Laughter.]

Senator COONS. Absolutely, Madam President. You are the President. You can do what you want. [Laughter.]

Technically, what we are doing from a parliamentary procedural perspective is that we are now going to conclude what was a meeting of the subcommittee, and I will now gavel in a formal hearing of the Senate Foreign Relations Subcommittee on African Affairs, which is the final hearing of this subcommittee for the 113th Congress.

And without objection, at the outset I would like to request the testimony from Save the Children and Catholic Relief Services be entered into the record. Additionally, I will request that a statement from the chairman of our full committee, Chairman Bob Menendez, be entered into the record.

[EDITOR'S NOTE.—The articles mentioned above can be found in the "Additional Material Submitted for the Record" section at the end of this hearing.]

Senator COONS. I would like to invite our four witnesses for our next panel to come forward while I make some brief opening remarks.

We plan to focus today on the factors that made it so easy for the Ebola virus to spread in West Africa and so difficult for it to be contained. It is by learning how we got here that I think we will be better able to prevent flareups and future outbreaks of Ebola and other highly infectious deadly diseases and reduce the likelihood that American and international intervention will again be necessary.

Ebola to date, in this outbreak in three countries in West Africa and several others, has claimed the lives of more than 6,000 men, women and children that we know of, and has infected nearly three times that many, mostly in Guinea, Liberia, and Sierra Leone, and has claimed the lives of 330 health workers, who I was pleased to see earlier today were recognized by Time Magazine as person of the year. It is often the unsung, unheralded men and women who took to this challenge on the ground and from throughout the world who I think we should be lifting up and supporting in the weeks and months ahead.

The international community, as we all know, was slow to respond to the outbreak and is still working to catch up, but the U.S. Government has already invested more than $780 million in the Ebola response effort, nearly twice the amount of the next largest donor, and I am grateful for the leadership actions of President Obama to ensure that members of our Armed Forces and the United States Uniform Public Health Service have been deployed and made available.

My understanding is that as of this week, roughly 2,600 U.S. Armed Forces and public health personnel are deployed in West Africa.

Our contributions are having a marked impact, as you heard from President Sirleaf. U.S. support for the establishment of Ebola treatment units and safe burial teams have contributed to a significant reduction in the rate of growth of the disease. However, our work is indeed far from done. Sierra Leone has seen a sharp rise in recent cases, and as cases continue to grow, Sierra Leone has surpassed Liberia, which previously for months had had the highest caseload. As we have heard from President Sirleaf, Liberia is still wrestling with this virus but is making very hopeful progress. Mali also recently saw its first Ebola cases in October and now has eight.

Ebola is a volatile virus with the potential to flare up at a moment's notice, and we need to be able to react as quickly as possible to contain it. So I hope we will talk about how we work together with our partners to ensure that we are prepared for future outbreaks and that we build at the ground level the public health resources that we need.

The U.S. Government was the first international governance institution to step in when the NGO community, which had been on the ground for months and truly led the response to Ebola, called for our response. It is because the United States stepped in, and at the scale we did, that progress has been made in combating this terrible disease. This is, as others have said, not just a matter of our national security, it is a matter of fundamental humanity.

We cannot as a country go back to the sidelines and watch these already impoverished and unstable countries fall apart when we as a nation have the resources and the calling to help turn this crisis around. I am elated to have heard from Appropriations Committee leadership that $5.4 billion in emergency funding is included in the appropriations package that will be taken up and voted on this week by the Senate of the United States to contribute to the pace and scale and investment required to not just control this outbreak but to invest in preventing future outbreaks.

The four witnesses who join us here today represent organizations that were fighting this Ebola outbreak far before headlines appeared here in the United States and have done heroic work for which all of us should be grateful.

Before I turn this over to my friend and distinguished ranking member, I just wanted to note what a pleasure it has been for me to chair this subcommittee these last 4 years. I have had the honor of sharing this dais over many hearings with two wonderful ranking members, Senator Isakson of Georgia and Senator Flake of Arizona, who care deeply and passionately about Africa and with whom it has been a true joy to work.

Senator Flake.

OPENING STATEMENT OF HON. JEFF FLAKE,
U.S. SENATOR FROM ARIZONA

Senator FLAKE. Thank you, Senator Coons, and let me just return the sentiment. It is wonderful to work with a chairman who not only cares deeply about the continent but has so much experience and firsthand knowledge and a desire to learn more all the time, and it has truly been a pleasure working with you, and I look forward to a long-time partnership on these issues. I want to thank you for calling this hearing as well, and for your response on this issue early on and encouraging a more robust response from the United States. I think the response that we have seen is, in large measure, due to your efforts. So, thank you for that, and thanks for this hearing.

I appreciate the witnesses being here and look forward to hearing what you have to say. As Senator Coons mentioned, there is a significant investment that has been made by the United States and the taxpayers, and we represent them. We want to make sure that the hard-earned funds that are being spent here are done so wisely. So that is why we are so anxious to hear from you on what we need to do, one, for the current crisis, and moving ahead what we need to do to make sure that we do not have flareups as well.

So, thank you for being here, look forward to the testimony.

Senator COONS. Thank you, Senator Flake.

I would now like to turn it over to our witnesses to make opening statements, and I will offer a brief introduction of each of you in turn.

First is Dr. Paul Farmer, one of the founders of Partners in Health. Dr. Farmer has been a revolutionary voice in public health globally and in working to build and sustain community-based health care institutions since the 1980s. He heads the Department of Global Health and Social Medicine at Harvard Medical School. Partners in Health had a footprint in West Africa prior to this outbreak, and Dr. Farmer has been on the front lines of soliciting international support for the Ebola response effort, and I am grateful for his passionate voice around the questions of equity and access to health care globally.

Dr. Anne Peterson is the vice dean of the Public Health Program at Ponce Health Services University and is former director of Global Health for World Vision and former USAID Assistant Administrator for the Bureau of Global Health. Dr. Peterson recently returned from Liberia and Sierra Leone, where she was working through World Vision to identify gaps in response efforts and evaluating how stakeholders have been coordinating efforts on the ground.

Mr. Pape Gaye is the president and CEO of IntraHealth International, which is focused on strengthening health systems by training health care workers in developing countries at the community level. A native of Senegal, Mr. Gaye has been a lifelong advocate of health systems strengthening in developing countries and now more than ever can speak to the needs in these crisis-stricken countries.

And last but certainly not least, Javier Alvarez is the Liberia country director for Mercy Corps, with more than 15 years of experience at UNDP and UNICEF, and he is an expert on humanitarian emergency response and wrote Mercy Corps' most recent report on the economic impact of Ebola in Liberia.

Thank you, all of you, for your service, for your time, for your advice, and we look forward to your input.

Dr. Farmer.

STATEMENT OF PAUL FARMER, M.D., COFOUNDER, PARTNERS IN HEALTH, BOSTON, MA

Dr. FARMER. Thank you, Mr. Chairman. Thank you, Senators. And greetings, Madam President. It is wonderful to see you, and thank you for the warm welcome that you have showed our teams in Liberia, and the leadership that you have shown in responding.

I am making just very brief and illustrative comments and will submit a more extensive written comment to the record, if that is acceptable to you, Senator.

Senator COONS. Without objection.

Dr. FARMER. I just wanted to—and I apologize for obliterating it. I do not know if there is an image that comes up. I would rather look at the President myself. But just as a reminder, the matter of zoonoses—that is, diseases that leap from animals to humans— is an important one. It will remain important. In the 1960s and 1970s and 1980s, some of these hemorrhagic fevers were first described, and remember HIV shortly thereafter, also a zoonosis which spread into a global pandemic. I believe this is what we are here to avert with a much more rapid, clinically rapid pathogen, Ebola.

Now, one of the questions that I was asked to address was how did this disease spread quickly. Every time there is an epidemic, there are explanatory voids where lots of assertions are made, and we heard in this example a great deal about bush meat and other exotic modes of transmission. We should be very clear that the rapid spread of Ebola is not due to 15,000 episodes of bush meat eating frenzy but rather to person-to-person transmission in a set- ting of weak health care infrastructure. So the diagnosis, speaking as a physician, is that it is critical that we understand that. So, weak health systems are responsible for the spread.

In interviewing survivors—these are three young people from Sierra Leone, but it is not a different story elsewhere in the region—there are very few mysteries. These are people who are looking after members of their families—their family members— while they are sick or after they have died. As in every culture in the world, we respect the dead, we bury the dead. That is actually in my faith tradition one of the corporeal works of mercy, if I get my Sunday school memory back, bury the dead. Of course, this is not something that can be easily wished away, that people stop re- vering those who have passed away and honoring them. So these are, as has been said, in a way, the heroes of the epidemic.

Now, what I hope we will be able to focus on in the hearing is what usually does not happen with emergency responses. The last time I was in this room was shortly after the earthquake in Haiti, making these very same points, and yet President Sirleaf has made them more effectively. We need to address the human resources for health crises. We need to build local capacity, local systems, and local health care infrastructure. That is how we will avert the next disaster.

This has gone under the unglamorous name of health systems strengthening. I think we need a consultant to help us think of something—you know, we all of us talk that language, but we need a little help from you. These are substantial resources you have requested, and we are thrilled to see that many of them will go into health systems strengthening that has a significant component focused on building local capacity in places that include Liberia, Sierra Leone, and Guinea.

I would like to just close by saying I personally am proud, as an American, of the CDC's role, the NIH, other American institutions that have stepped up. I think I am very grateful for my colleagues who are physicians and nurses from the states you represent and all across the country who have gone in to serve Partners in Health, who is proud to be part of this coalition. We will seek to promote health systems strengthening while we are looking for the new and sexier term and to open with our colleagues in the public health sector in Liberia and Sierra Leone—and we hope one day Guinea—many clinical units able to take care of people sick with Ebola.

But also, as noted, and maybe I skipped over this, the largest number of Ebola victims will not have Ebola. They will have malaria, they will have obstructive labor, they will have minor injuries that, because there is no health care system, will fester and take their lives or maim them in other ways.

So we are looking forward to responding over the course of the coming years and again are grateful to the President for being here with us today, but also for being such a welcoming host. Thank you.

[The prepared statement in the form of slides of Dr. Farmer follows:]

Slow Plague vs. Fast Plague?

Zoonoses from equatorial Africa

- Marburg, Germany (1967)
- Yambuku, Zaire (1976)
- Nzara, Sudan (1976)

Photo by Lyle Conrad

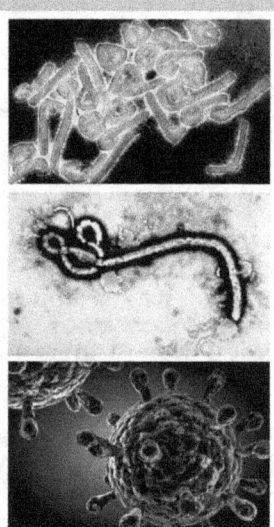

15

How Did Ebola Spread So Quickly?

Ebola As A Caregivers' Disease

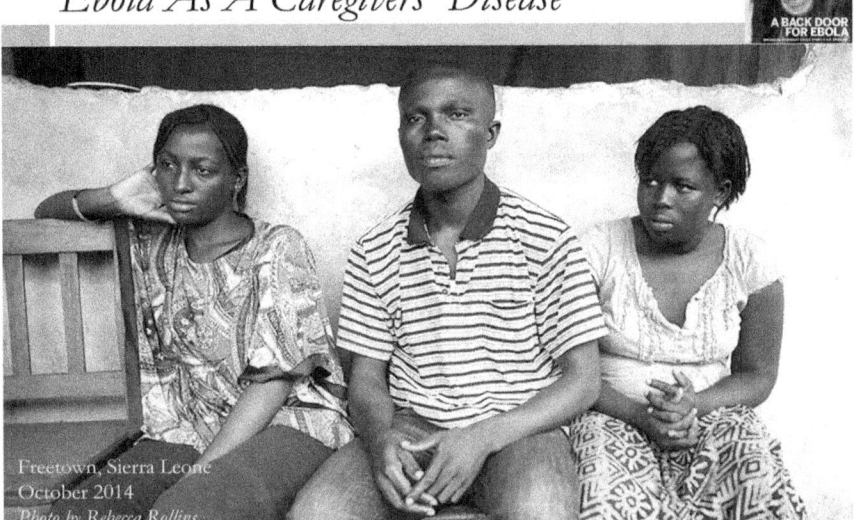

Freetown, Sierra Leone
October 2014
Photo by Rebecca Rollins

EBOLA RESPONSE COALITION
SIERRA LEONE AND LIBERIA

 **Partners In Health** EBOLA RESPONSE

TARGETS *for* JANUARY 1, 2015

30	2,400	500	5,000	60-80
clinics and facilities	daily patients	local clinical and non-clinical support staff	community health workers	expatriate clinicians in Liberia and Sierra Leone

Two Tasks, One Team
Respond to Ebola, Build/Rebuild Health Systems

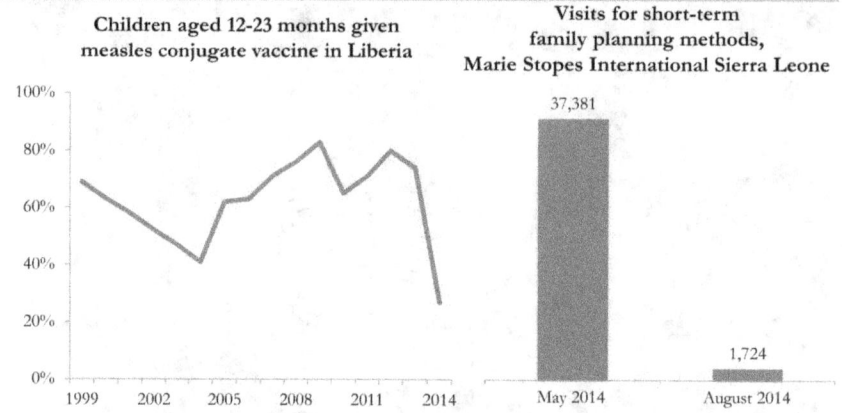

Children aged 12-23 months given
measles conjugate vaccine in Liberia

Visits for short-term
family planning methods,
Marie Stopes International Sierra Leone

WHO. Vaccine-Preventable Diseases Monitoring System: 2014 Update.

Hamilton J. "Ebola Is Preventing Kids from Getting Vaccinated in Liberia." NPR: October 23, 2014.

UNFPA Sierra Leone Country Office. Impact of Ebola Outbreak on Reproductive Health and Proposed Mitigation Strategy. October 2014.

What Never Happens with Emergency Responses?

HUMAN RESOURCES
FOR HEALTH PROGRAM
REPUBLIC OF RWANDA

- Health systems strengthening

- Training/capacity building

- Research

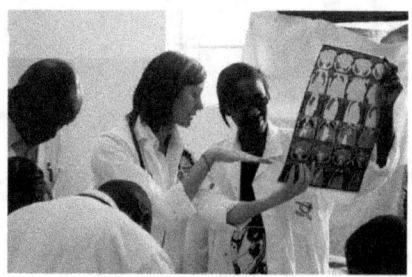

What Would This Look Like?

Photo by Partners In Health.   Photo by Partners In Health.

Senator COONS. Thank you, Dr. Farmer.

For several members of the subcommittee who have joined us, the President of Liberia made remarks previously and has graciously agreed to stay and to hear from our witnesses.

Dr. Anne Peterson.

Dr. Peterson.

STATEMENT OF E ANNE PETERSON, M.D., VICE DEAN, PUBLIC HEALTH PROGRAM, PONCE HEALTH SCIENCES UNIVERSITY, WORLD VISION, WASHINGTON, DC

Dr. PETERSON. Thank you, Chairman Coons and Ranking Member Flake, and subcommittee members as well; and thank you for having this hearing and for inviting me to be here.

I went to Liberia and Sierra Leone not so much to look at what was being done well—and I will say many things are being done very well in all of the countries, and especially in the United States response—but my terms of reference as I went with World Vision was to look at what are the gaps, what are the gaps between what the faith communities are doing or could be doing and how well are they working together with the U.S. Government.

So I will try to focus my remarks on six areas where I think we could do a little better than we have. Three of them are in areas of ongoing effort, and the first is in the need for cross-cutting coordination.

If you talk to anyone who is working on the ground, they will tell you there is a lot of coordination happening. There are meetings and meetings and pillar meetings and coordination meetings. But they are all focused in their more narrow vertical programming. We have seen this all along in health development. Vertical programs, vertical efforts can be very, very effective. But when you do that, you do not build an intact health system. So as I went and looked across the pillars, across government agencies and NGOs and faith-based organizations, as I looked at the difference between what was happening in Liberia and Sierra Leone, in fact there were a number of places where it was clear that if we had had a bigger view, a cross-cutting collaboration and coordination, we would have had economies of scale, we would have had reduced duplication, and some of the gaps in what needs to have been done would not have been missed.

So my first call was outlined in the Institute of Medicine report that was published this summer, "Investing in Global Health Systems: Sustaining Gains and Transforming Lives," that I was honored to cochair with Ambassador John Lang. We talked about this need to go from vertical focus to a broad health systems approach, and the same thing is happening right now in Ebola response, and we can do better than that.

The next is to invest sustainably. Very rightly, investments that the U.S. Government and others are putting in are focused on stopping Ebola. Stopping Ebola is absolutely essential. But we are also setting it up in such a way that the ground is being cleared, the tents are being put up, the labs are set, the foreign doctors and health care workers are coming in, and when Ebola is done, my desperate fear is that the tents will be rolled up and the expats will go home, and what will be left will be the previous health system that is only more broken than before Ebola came.

So as we are doing just what we should be doing in addressing Ebola, if we could focus on investing it so that it will make permanent improvements in the health systems; to be, in fact, training and building health worker capacity even as we deal with the Ebola epidemic itself.

My third "do it better" comment is in the area of listening to communities. Communities are part of the health system. If, in fact, we do not hear their needs and address their needs, they do not respond to our behavior change messages. So we heard from President Sirleaf that people heard messages that this is a terrible disease, it is a fatal disease. Well, if that is so, then why would you send your child to disappear into an Ebola treatment unit and never come home? Instead, we should be looking at what can be done, celebrating survivors, knowing that people can protect themselves, protect their families. By going in sooner when they have Ebola, they can prevent transmission to their families.

So I would ask that all of the communities and the collaboration that is going on, do not just talk to one another. Remember to go in and talk to the people of communities. Some of the best messages I heard were talking to mothers in the slum communities in Monrovia and Freetown, and I will tell you I am not surprised that in Freetown, in Sierra Leone, cases are going up. It is exactly what I expected as I looked at both the economic issues and the behavioral issues and Ebola approaching those slum dwellings.

So there are now three game changers, and I am almost out of time. You probably have not heard about rapid diagnostic tests as a major game changer. I will tell you that if we could distinguish between who has Ebola and who does not have Ebola, you would change how many people are in the Ebola units, and you would be able to remove those from risk who do not have Ebola, the malarias that look like Ebola. You would change the ability of health care workers to go in and man the regular outpatient departments so we could begin to address the indirect impacts and profound health impacts of other diseases, and we would change what happens in burials.

Maybe up to 70 percent of community transmission is now happening in funerals and burials. If people knew when someone died whether they truly were an Ebola patient or not, we would then have fewer Ebola burials. We would not be doing Ebola burials with destruction of homes for those who are not Ebola patients. So for me, the rapid diagnostic test is a profound game changer in almost every aspect, and it would stop a lot of transmission.

The last and probably most important, if we are going to listen to communities and learn from them, we need to work with the faith-based sector. They are the link between our governments, our NGOs, and the communities. They know where the orphans are, they know where the people in need are, and they are an incredible vehicle. There are starting to be quite a number of things. World Vision is doing safe burials, but dignified and safe burials, meeting the cultural needs of the people.

In closing, I will just say that I would suggest that we need to focus on listening better, building back better, partnering with the communities and the faith-based organizations; and I, like Dr. Farmer, am very pleased and very proud of the work that the U.S. Government has been doing in West Africa.

Thank you.

[The prepared statement of Dr. Peterson follows:]

PREPARED STATEMENT OF DR. E ANNE PETERSON

Chairman Coons, Ranking Member Flake, and subcommittee members, thank you for conducting this hearing on what remains a critical issue to Americans and to the people of West Africa. Thank you also for the honor of being able to speak with you about Ebola. I have spoken before this committee previously when I was Assistant Administrator for Global Health at USAID, but now hopefully will bring a civil society and on the ground perspective on what is and could be done to address Ebola in the affected countries.

Recently, I spent most of a month first in Liberia and then in Sierra Leone as a consultant to World Vision. My terms of reference for that consultancy were very similar to the questions to be discussed in this hearing. I was to assess what was being done, what could be done better and what additional capacity was needed to meet the gaps. The focus of the assessment was on what the faith sector was contributing to the response. My broad terms of reference connected me with a variety of government agencies (U.S. Ambassador in Liberia, CDC, USAID, DFID, and both national Ministry of Heath representatives) as well as a myriad of NGO, FBOs, and individual faith leaders. We were able to see an incredible amount of what was happening in response to Ebola could spend time with people in communities in both the countries we visited. This gave us a big picture view of the response but also gave us access to the community perspective that highlighted strengths, weaknesses, gaps and growing needs that had not been addressed yet.

I would like to focus my testimony on three areas of current work that I believe could be enhanced, three "game changers" and then some suggestions about how future USG investments might be prioritized to speed ending the Ebola crisis, mitigate the suffering of the countries most impacted and help rebuild the health system so that Ebola or other similar crises never take hold again at this level. Let me say first and strongly, that the emphasis on stopping Ebola is the correct focus and there is a great effort to achieve that end, but there is room to work smarter and to greater effect. The international aid community is fully aware of the need for coordination, correct messaging and need to build health care capacity but the workload and vertical pillar approach have limited the perspective and effectiveness in each of these areas. With some new perspectives the current work could be significantly more effective. Some of these needed changes were beginning to happen as I left Africa but clarity and encouragement to continue those improvements will maximize impact and the usefulness of the U.S. investments in Ebola. The three game changers would be (1) engagement and mobilization of the faith community;

(2) availability of a rapid Ebola test; and (3) addressing now the massive indirect impacts of Ebola on the economy, society, and health of the impacted countries. Each of these "game changers" would significantly help reduce transmission of Ebola and mitigate the immediate and long term harm of the epidemic, beginning to reestablish a stable, functional system.

ACHIEVING GREATER IMPACT IN OUR CURRENT EFFORTS

There are several ways that the current Ebola epidemic response could be improved to achieve greater impact, both in the immediate and the long term.

First, there is a need for cross-cutting coordination. Coordination of effort is essential and a great deal of time and energy is appropriately being expended on coordination with national government and collaborating aid agencies. While the current coordination is essential the intensity of the response work and the narrow focus of work within each of the coordinating pillars leaves little time for collaborating across pillars, agencies or even learning lessons from nearby affected countries. Opportunities for synergy are lost, unnecessary duplication of effort is inevitable. These are predictably inefficiencies and like vertical programming of the past measureable and laudable progress might be happening in a certain "pillar" of the response, but the disconnected pillars do not build a coherent health system. The gaps between the vertical pillars are no one's responsibility and go unnoticed until they reach harmful levels. The recent Institute of Medicine (IOM) report that I was honored to cochair with Ambassador John Lange, "Investing in Global Health Systems: Sustaining Gains, Transforming Lives," speaks about the limitation of the piecemeal approach to health and cites this Ebola outbreak as an example of what happens without a strong and intact health system. Our Ebola response is falling into a similar vertical, piecemeal set of actions.

Invest sustainably. The U.S. is investing heavily in the Ebola response and doing good Ebola control response with the invested funds. It is probably necessary, at least for patient care, that there is a parallel Ebola system in addition to the regular health care infrastructure. We do want to separate Ebola patients from other patients to prevent transmission. We are clearing land, putting up tents, and manning Ebola units primarily with foreign medical personnel. While this is due in part to an existing lack of health care workforce exacerbated by the epidemic, it is not an approach that will help build national capacity, either in health facilities or workforce. When Ebola has been halted, the tents will be rolled up and removed, the foreign workers will return home. The other preventable health problems that have been ignored and neglected by a health system either shut down or diverted to Ebola will be of far larger proportions than before Ebola emerged. And unless we do our current work differently, the health system which has lost so much manpower will be weaker than before Ebola while forced to address greater and ongoing health challenges. It is possible, to address the urgent Ebola scale-up needs in a way that contributes to a stronger and sustainable health system. If we plan and invest only in the short-term control of Ebola, we will miss a great opportunity to strengthen national health systems to build their capacity to address the already prevalent preventable maternal and child deaths or to avert or respond to the next major health crisis.

Listen to the communities. There are so many meetings and long conversations among all the Ebola response agencies that it isn't obvious initially that conversations are primarily between foreign aid workers and the government officials and rarely do we hear the voice of community members. Decisions and activities in the Ebola response have in some cases led to distrust and anger in communities, messages on the seriousness of Ebola have been scoffed at as unreal by some and taken fatalistically by others. In many instances, well intentioned scientifically based messages just haven't elicited the behavioral responses from the communities that were desired and transmission of Ebola therefore continues. The only way to develop effective behavior change programs and messages is to know and address the issues of the community from their perspective, addressing the fears and beliefs that have hindered the response effort. Listening before messaging is the key. Listening to the concerns of community members, the mothers with young children as well as leaders who might be at the decision tables will lead to a better understanding of what is needed to change behaviors and reduce Ebola transmission.

GAME CHANGER: ENGAGING WITH THE FAITH COMMUNITY

If most Ebola transmission is happening in communities, as it is, and if we acknowledge it is hard for foreign aid agencies to link directly to communities, then an interface or intervening organization is needed. Far better than secular NGOs, faith-based NGOs or FBOs and church or Muslim associations are deeply embedded and knowledgeable about their communities and can link the voices and views of the communities to the Ebola response.

The U.S. Government has long worked with faith-based organizations. Engaging with FBOs was critical in the war against AIDS and rose to some prominence in the implementation of PEPFAR. Longer ago than PEPFAR, local churches were instrumental in the small pox eradication efforts in the same West African settings now beset by Ebola. Yet, USG engagement with FBOs or mobilization of the faith networks has not been a core part of the Ebola response to date.

A core focus of my work in Liberia and Sierra Leone was to conduct a qualitative assessment for World Vision of the roles of faith-based organizations (FBOs), churches and faith leaders in the Ebola response; what were they doing, what could they be doing and how could they be better integrated with the U.S. Government Ebola response. Granted, there are fewer FBOs who work in disaster humanitarian operations type settings, but there are some FBOs experienced, willing or active, such as Samaritan's Purse work in Liberia that responded early and at great cost in establishing Ebola treatment centers. Medical Teams International is providing training in infection control. Catholic Relief Services, CAFOD (another Catholic FBO), Catholic Medical Mission Board, MAP international, IMA World Health and World Vision all are participating in different places and ways.

I'll use World Vision as just one example of what FBOs can contribute to the fight against Ebola. World Vision works primarily in Sierra Leone and has taken on unusual leadership roles in addressing Ebola, such as efforts to improve safe and dignified burials, training pastors and imams on Ebola prevention and stigma reduction, and addressing the indirect consequences of Ebola (including food insecurity, livelihoods, care of orphans and survivors, and educating children while they are out of school).

The first and perhaps most urgent FBO coalition activity was taking on safe and dignified burials. The World Vision coalition in Sierra Leone, with Catholic and Muslims partners, has taken on managing, training, and paying burial teams in 12 of the14 districts. They are making sure the Ministry of Health burial teams are actually paid for their gruesome work, using their financial management expertise. As result of this effort, there are fewer burial team strikes and great progress has been made toward responding and conducting all burials within 24 hours.

The added value of the FBO rather than secular coalition is that they have added a strong emphasis on how to convert safe but offensive burial practices (mass unmarked graves, no markers, no prayers or family attendance) into safe but dignified burials acceptable to the communities. As burials become "dignified" and faithful to spiritual traditions, families will no longer need to conduct the high risk transmission secret burials of Ebola deaths that are occurring now.

But the issue isn't just what are international FBOs doing but what are the faith leaders and local churches doing and what part could they play in the Ebola response in their communities. In Liberia, there was more vigorous infection control but less visible coordination among the faith community. The reverse was true in Sierra Leone, where infection control practices were more lax but there was more action and greater coordination among the local faith community.

The church, as has been true in past epidemics like AIDS, has been mixed in their response. There are many examples of churches being helpful and others that spread messages and practices contrary to helping control the spread of infection and discourage stigma. The situation is improving over time as the stark reality of Ebola hits congregations directly. Most churches have stopped the practice of greeting one another with handshakes or kisses or "laying on of hands" in prayer for the sick. Many, but not all, churches and mosques now have chlorine and hand-washing stations set up before people enter the church though sometimes the chlorine is missing and the water bucket is dry. A brave few churches were venturing out from their church buildings to conduct services right outside the doors of Ebola treatment units so patients can hear that others are praying for them. Others are beginning to note and address the needs of widows and orphans, or provide trauma counseling for devastated families. Support and reassurance from faith leaders is essential also in helping the transition to safe and dignified burials be acceptable to their communities. If faith leaders are engaged and informed they can even pave the way for acceptance of new tools, like an Ebola vaccine or rapid diagnostic test once they are available.

The faith community has a clear command to meet the needs of their people, but as the epidemic has spread, the desire for reliable information has grown but many churches and mosques do not have reliable ways to learn about Ebola to correctly guide their congregations. Some have welcomed scientists from the CDC to their services to learn about Ebola. In addition to information from the government and CDC, there is a need to frame the science of Ebola response into the more familiar faith language of the Christians and Muslims. World Vision is leading another consortium, working with CRS and the Muslim organization Focus 1000, on the production of a toolkit on Ebola messaging to be disseminated through the leaders of each faith group. World Vision is combining the available scientific information on Ebola with the faith oriented tool kit into a reflective and action oriented training for a wide array of faith leaders, Muslim and Christian, through its Channels of Hope program which had previously been developed and used for training in HIV/AIDS.

Through this tool, faith leaders can reduce negative messages and enhance positive ones, such as that reporting in to Ebola centers as soon as the disease is suspected protects their families from harm. Rather than preaching fear, faith leaders can affirm that God works through His people to meet the needs of the sick, widows, and orphans. Framing the stigma being experienced by families of victims and survivors in parallel to biblical example of reaching out and caring for lepers and outcasts can be particularly helpful in reducing stigma faced by survivors. Correct information, in the hands of faith leaders, harmonized and expressed in their faith language, can overcome widespread mistrust of the government and by extension the Ebola response. FBOs and faith leaders can encourage the people of Liberia, Sierra Leone, and Guinea not only to respond more appropriately to Ebola but to be active agents to stop the spread of Ebola and mitigate the enormous personal, spiritual, and societal impacts of Ebola on their people.

But the impact of Ebola and the opportunities for faith leaders and FBOs to mitigate the impact of Ebola goes far beyond stopping Ebola infections. Food insecurity is increasing as prices rise and farmers are not planting crops. Attention is also diverted from other health issues. Most deaths in Ebola-affected countries are not Ebola deaths. The even larger epidemic of deaths is from pneumonia, childbirth, malaria, and diarrhea due to the Ebola epidemic's impact on the health care system, lack of preventive services and broken societal and economic structures. Addressing these issues cannot wait for the end of the Ebola outbreak and the global health community, FBOs and faith leaders know how to prevent these deaths. It is the kind of work they are already called to do. They just need encouragement and resources to take on the daunting devastation of the impact of Ebola on these countries.

GAME CHANGER: RAPID DIAGNOSTIC TEST FOR EBOLA

Ebola symptoms are similar initially to many other diseases. This nonspecificity of symptoms has profound impacts on health care worker risk and on patient care seeking behavior. I would argue that not being able to know promptly whether a patient (or body) has Ebola or not is a major driver of continued Ebola transmission and the cause of the collapse of almost all other health services, leading to unmeasured numbers of non-Ebola deaths indirectly caused by Ebola. A rapid diagnostic test would have a dramatic impact on both health care workers and patients

Most of the recent health care worker infections have not occurred in Ebola treatment centers but in settings where they thought they were treating illnesses other than Ebola. A doctor was infected and died after delivering a baby. Forty-two health workers were infected by one Ebola patient, a friend who claimed initially only to have an ulcer. Twenty one of those health workers died. Each time a health care worker in a non-Ebola center is infected and diagnosed as an Ebola patient, all his or her health care worker colleagues become contacts, must be quarantined and often the care center closes until the 21-day quarantine is completed. Perhaps as much as two-thirds of the regular health system is closed and once closed, it is very hard for health care workers to return to take on again the risks of caring for patients who are not supposed to have Ebola but might.

Patients, just like doctors, can't tell the initial Ebola symptoms apart from many other common diseases. Unless they have had significant exposure to a sick or dead Ebola patient, most of the symptoms will be due to malaria, diarrhea, typhoid fever, lassa fever or the number one child killer, pneumonia. These very common illnesses, have only become more common as the immunization programs, malaria prevention programs, outpatient treatment centers have closed in mass. Mothers, in poor slum areas have stated emphatically, that if they or their child was sick with a fever or a stomach ache or diarrhea they would not bring them in to a treatment center. They know these symptoms could be Ebola, but they believe sometimes rightly and sometimes with wishful thinking, that it is far more likely to not be Ebola than to be Ebola. They don't want to risk "disappearing into an Ebola" center never to return. When someone becomes sick they are rightly afraid to come in for care. If their symptoms could at all be like Ebola, as is true of many common illnesses, they know they will be held in Ebola observation until the test result is known 2–3 or more days later. They also know that staying in these holding centers with suspected

Ebola cases puts them at high risk of being infected with Ebola while seeking care for another health problem. Very logically they stay home until it is clear they have Ebola. They would rather risk their child dying at home of malaria than risk getting Ebola and dying far away.

But if in fact, the sick person has Ebola the delay in accessing care has impact on more than just that one individual. We have learned in this epidemic that Ebola is both more infectious as the disease progresses and that infectivity is dose dependent. The sicker and longer an Ebola patient stays in the home the greater the likelihood of transmission to family and friends.

But if we had a rapid Ebola test at the triage of all non-Ebola centers and maybe even available for community health workers, all of these scenarios are changed. Health care workers could safely go back to work and families could safely bring their sick family members in for diagnosis and treatment. Communities, families, and patients would know only non-Ebola patients would be in the regular health centers and Ebola patients would be referred to now much less crowded Ebola centers. This would decrease transmission of Ebola in communities because families would be less likely to delay. It would decrease transmission within holding and quarantine centers. Patients could safely seek treatment for malaria and the increasing common diseases caused directly by the diversion of care to Ebola and halting of preventive and curative services other than Ebola. It would even reduce transmission in Ebola centers where uninfected suspect cases were previously being exposed to Ebola. Health care workers, both national and international volunteers, who are not ready to treat Ebola but do want to assist with the devastating health needs in the impacted countries could safely return to work. We could begin to rebuild the broken health system that allow the Ebola rampage to begin and continue unchecked.

Community Ebola burials have been a source of anger and sometimes violence, especially if it turns out the death was not an Ebola death. A rapid test would contribute rebuilding of relationships with the community and to decreasing transmission since only the fewer and proven Ebola burials would need Ebola burials. If secret burials were thereby avoided, we would begin to get more accurate death reporting, surveillance, and referral. It would also help ensure when there is a non-Ebola death that homes and possessions aren't destroyed unnecessarily. A rapid diagnostic test would facilitate more rapid access to care for family contacts, less breaking of quarantine and fewer contacts lost to followup. All of these impacts will lead to better data on deaths, reduced burial transmission and better relationships with community members, which directly or indirectly enhances Ebola infection control.

GAME CHANGER: ADDRESS THE INDIRECT IMPACTS OF EBOLA

The massive indirect impacts of Ebola on the economy, education, social structures and health of the impacted countries are much greater and long-lasting than the impact of the Ebola epidemic itself. The plight of children demonstrates just a portion of this impact. WHO estimate of the number of orphans from October 29 for the three countries was 10,395 single orphans and 4,455 double orphans. These numbers corrected for underreporting (CDC uses 2.5 fold multiplier, which has been verified in an active surveillance activity in November) would make the estimated total orphans 25,986. Because of the previous civil war, there were many single parented homes in both Liberia and Sierra Leone. When Ebola hits these vulnerable homes, with perhaps greater adult vulnerability to Ebola than children, there are a disproportionate number of double orphans which is unprecedented even in Africa. In Sierra Leone, 42 percent of the orphans are double orphans and in some districts there were more double orphans (both parents dead) than single orphans. This was unheard of even in the height of the AIDS epidemic.

Life is difficult in Sierra Leone and Liberia, even before Ebola. There are high child and maternal mortality rates and poverty in both countries, which was just beginning to improve after the civil war of a decade ago. Now, ALL children are impacted by Ebola. Most are out of school for the entire year, with some radio broadcast classes as their only educational input. About 50 percent of parents have been keeping their children home—all the time—no friends, no family gatherings, so they aren't exposed to Ebola. Most of the regular health care facilities are closed for any usual illnesses—malaria, diarrhea, pneumonia. Children (all children but even more so for orphans) are less well-nourished because of increasing poverty and food insecurity, they are also no longer receiving preventive services like Vitamin A or routine vaccinations. Therefore disease rates are escalating just as access to all health services, except Ebola services, are decreasing.

Stigma is a debilitating reality for children, adult survivors, and families of Ebola victims even if they never had Ebola. People are afraid of the children as potential vectors of Ebola but also don't trust that the children won't bring Ebola into their home, even after a 21 day quarantine. Unlike other orphan situations in Africa, the extended family is very reluctant to take the children in. Even those who would, usually can't afford to take in extra children. The economy is so hard hit with so many businesses and schools closed that there is little income. Families in poor urban areas have gone from two meals a day to one meal a day for their own children and just can't feed anymore. In rural areas, between stigma and lack of crops, orphaned children are abandoned in large numbers. People are also afraid of survivors, especially since even when a survivor is no longer infectious they often have continued symptoms of migratory joint and muscle pain—which people misinterpret as still sick with Ebola. Survivors often move across the country to avoid anyone knowing they were sick with Ebola even if they are fully recovered.

Often survivors also have no home to return to or family members have no home to stay in. When a sick person or body is picked up the house must be decontaminated, this may destroy much of the household belongings and the house itself is stigmatized as an Ebola house. It may in fact be infectious for a few days so care and decontamination is needed. But the process leads to further impoverishment and stigmatizing of those who have just been through the horrific experience of being sick with Ebola.

The indirect impacts of Ebola need immediate and long term response. Without food and financial support food insecurity now, is likely to evolve into something closer to famine in a few months. WFP, UNICEF, and some NGOs, like World Vision, are beginning to partner with faith leaders and communities to identify hard hit communities, orphans and other vulnerable children (OVC) and survivors to begin to provide child protection, food, and safe places to live.

These devastating impacts of Ebola warrant attention in their own right. These are illnesses and deaths we know well how to prevent. But ignoring them also impacts Ebola prevention efforts. Sick and malnourished children maybe more vulnerable to Ebola but certainly will add to the case load of an already overburdened health system. Every malaria case prevented is one less diagnostic dilemma that complicates isolation of suspected Ebola patients. When hunger, illness, or economic necessity compel someone to break quarantine more Ebola transmission is possible. When these other concerns loom so large and compromise life and health, Ebola precautions fall in relative importance and increased transmission becomes more likely. We cannot wait until the end of the Ebola outbreak massive indirect impacts of Ebola on West African society. Again, in Sierra Leone World Vision is ahead of the game in commissioning a rapid assessment of these indirect impacts of Ebola. They will use the information to help them reprogram their own funds but I believe this information will also provide desperately needed data for advocacy and prioritization of the global efforts.

What could/should the USG do?

- Stop Ebola by enlisting the assistance of those who care even more than we do—the people of Liberia, Sierra Leone, and Guinea. Work with trusted faith leaders to empower communities: listening to their concerns and potential solutions.
- Rebuild better not separate and temporary. The incredibly weak heath system, lack of surveillance systems, labs, inadequate workforce are the things that allowed the Ebola outbreak to reach such epic proportions. Instead of building a parallel system, in tents and manned by foreign health care workers, we should be ''building back better'' in ways that last; upgrading permanent facilities, building communications systems, training all cadres of health workers in infection control and disease treatment with a strong emphasis on preventive medicine, public health and community-based interventions and disease prevention. It would have been far easier to identify the first cases of Ebola if they were not lost among the many sick from diseases we know how to prevent.
- Don't wait. The indirect impacts of Ebola on the people of each of these countries are enormous. As poverty, malnutrition, lack of school and work and preventable diseases increase, Ebola control will fall lower on the population's priority list. If you can't feed your child, the ''far away'' risk of getting Ebola becomes much less important.
- Listen well, address their fears, give messages of hope, celebrate survivors, and empower parents, families and communities to protect themselves and assist in the response.
- Message at home. Stopping Ebola in Africa is the best protection for Americans and celebrate those willing to serve in Africa. Healthy people don't transmit

Ebola. Health care workers are not a danger to Americans just because they have worked in West Africa. We need to encourage American volunteers who want to help to be able to go and to be able to return home without stigma, shunning and exclusion from normal American work and society. The inappropriate level of fear is hindering the flow of aid workers needed to stop this Ebola epidemic there and increasing the risk of spread here.

CONCLUSION

I am very proud of my country for its extraordinary efforts to address Ebola. The investments by the U.S. to address the Ebola outbreak in West Africa are critical and are the best way to protect the American people. We have learned an immense amount in this current epidemic, that we couldn't have learned from previous smaller outbreaks. But we must continue to learn and to apply the lessons learned, to improving our medical and the nonmedical programs, addressing the urgent demands of stemming the spread of Ebola and addressing the urgent life needs of communities devastated by the presence of Ebola in their country We are doing well but we can do even better by investing in the right interventions, focusing on long-term sustainability and engaging the right stakeholders. We can stop the Ebola epidemic and leave behind a health system and developed infrastructure well-positioned to respond to future crises.

Senator COONS. Thank you, Dr. Peterson.
Mr. Gaye.

STATEMENT OF PAPE GAYE, PRESIDENT AND CEO, INTRAHEALTH INTERNATIONAL, CHAPEL HILL, NC

Mr. GAYE. Chairman Coons, Ranking Member Flake, and other distinguished members of the subcommittee, on behalf of Intra-Health International, I thank you for inviting me to testify today on this issue of paramount importance to our friends in West Africa and to us here in the United States.

I ask that my full written testimony be submitted for the record.

Senator COONS. Without objection.

Mr. GAYE. In my native Senegal, there is a Wolof proverb: "Nit, nit ay garabam." It means "the best medicine for a person is another person." I am fortunate to lead an organization, IntraHealth International, that for 35 years has been a firsthand witness to this proverb in action through our support to frontline health workers in 100 countries around the world, including all the Ebola-affected countries.

Tragically, however, far too many people in the West Africa region I hold dear did not have access to that person, that health worker, who could have prevented Ebola from decimating their communities and threatening the well-being and security of their countries, their region, and the world.

As this Ebola outbreak has already started to fade from the consciousness of some, one of the crucial underlying conditions that helped the virus spread remains the absence of a sustainable and resilient health workforce in the region. Let there be no misunderstanding: if health workforce does not get the high-level political attention it sorely needs, workforce deficiencies will continue to threaten global health security, and threaten the tremendous progress made in saving women and children's lives, fighting diseases like HIV/AIDS, and all the great work accomplished by USAID.

As shared by President Sirleaf, Liberia, Sierra Leone, and Guinea all had fewer than three doctors, nurses, and midwives per 10,000 people, even before the Ebola epidemic began. But these countries are hardly alone. The World Health Organization last year estimated that 83 countries in the world are below the minimum threshold of health workers needed to provide essential services to everyone.

Last year, at a major conference in Brazil, Guinea and Liberia were among 57 countries that made health workforce commitments. Guinea's commitment highlighted two rural provinces where frontline health workers were largely absent, and one of those regions is where "Patient Zero" of the Ebola epidemic was believed to be infected less than a month later.

Let me be clear: because of the generosity of the American people and the know-how and innovations of implementing partners like IntraHealth, the United States Government has maintained global health leadership, and no one on this Earth will dispute that the mantle of that leadership rests and will continue to rest on the shoulders of the United States.

For example, IntraHealth and UNICEF are currently working with the Liberian government on a tool called mHero to allow the Ministry of Health and health workers to instantly communicate critical information. The USAID-supported, open-source, online personnel management system, called iHRIS, will save low-income countries about $232 million, and data using the tool has already been used to drive additional domestic investment for health workers. In the next 5 years, iHRIS is expected to save the Liberian Government, the equivalent amount of money as the salaries of 317 Liberian nurses. That number of nurses could serve 634,000 Liberians.

These innovations supported by American foreign assistance are critical to addressing some health workforce challenges, but certainly not all of them. The Frontline Health Workers Coalition, an alliance of 41 U.S.-based public and private organizations, with a Secretariat housed in our offices at IntraHealth, last month released recommendations for how the United States can lead on these issues. I have included them in an addendum to my testimony.

In brief, there must be a more concerted effort to address the needs of local health workers in West Africa, such as ensuring timely delivery of hazard pay and personal protective equipment. This support to local health workers must be backed by an equally fervent political push for addressing the most critical health workforce gaps globally. A 2010 report estimated that by 2020, the United States needs to invest at least $5.5 billion in health workforce strengthening to achieve its global health goals. Investment must be guided by a cross-agency strategy that sends an unequivocal message that America is committed to this issue, and we expect others to respond in kind. I also believe all global health procurements should be required to show how they will help strengthen the health workforce and systems.

I would like to close by asking each of us to think about what it would be like to wake up tomorrow morning infected with Ebola and not have a single person in your community to turn to for care, or to have your infant child this evening show signs of malaria and have nowhere to take them. This is the reality for far too many, and it must be changed now. We would be doing a great disservice to the 346 health workers who, as of the end of November, have given their lives to help turn the tide on this Ebola epidemic if we did not focus on their colleagues' immediate needs, while working fervently to ensure we never again have a crisis of this scale in public health.

I thank you very much, and I look forward to answering your questions.

[The prepared statement of Mr. Gaye follows:]

PREPARED STATEMENT OF PAPE GAYE

Chairman Coons, Ranking Member Flake, and other distinguished members of the subcommittee, on behalf of IntraHealth International, I would like to thank you for the honor of inviting me to testify today on this issue of paramount importance to the security and well-being of our friends in West Africa, as well as to us here in the United States. I ask that my full written testimony be submitted for the record.

In my native Senegal, there is a Wolof proverb, ''Nit, nit ay garabam.'' It means ''the best medicine for a person is another person.''

I am fortunate to lead an organization, IntraHealth International, which, for 35 years, has been a firsthand witness to this proverb in action through the awe-inspiring efforts of frontline health workers we have supported in 100 countries around the world, including all the Ebola-affected countries.

Tragically, however, far too many people in my native West Africa have not had access to that person—that health worker—who has the training and support necessary to prevent the Ebola virus from desolating their communities and threatening the well-being and security of their countries, their region, and the world.

Stories from this epidemic—such as the five Liberian children who were left at home with the corpses of their Ebola-infected parents for three days because of overwhelmed ambulance services—make us sick to our stomachs and heighten our resolve to end the crisis as soon as possible. The heroic efforts of health workers on the front lines of the epidemic have given us hope that, if our resolve to support them does not waiver, that day is coming soon.

But as this Ebola epidemic has already started to fade from the consciousness of some, one of the crucial underlying conditions that helps the virus spread remains: the absence of a sustainable and resilient global health workforce to both stop threats like Ebola in their tracks and complete the daily work of saving and making lives healthier in every community.

Let there be no misunderstanding: if health workforce deficiencies do not get the high-level political attention the issue sorely needs and it continues to languish as a global health policy afterthought, it will continue to threaten both global health security and the tremendous progress the United States has helped to lead in saving women's and children's lives and fighting diseases such as HIV/AIDS and tuberculosis.

Liberia, Sierra Leone, and Guinea all had fewer than three doctors, nurses, and midwives per 10,000 people even before the Ebola outbreak began. More people could very well die due to Ebola's impact on such fragile workforces and systems than directly from the Ebola virus itself. Yet, these countries are hardly alone. The World Health Organization last year estimated 83 countries are below the minimum threshold of 22.8 doctors, nurses, and midwives per 10,000 people needed to provide essential services to a population.

The countries that have the most acute workforce crises—the Ebola-affected countries in West Africa among them—have long recognized the gravity of inaction on health workforce strengthening for their communities, and they have been committed to action. Unfortunately, chronic lack of attention and significant reduction of formal development assistance to the West Africa region as a whole has exacerbated the problem.

Last year, I had the pleasure of speaking to government and civil society leaders and health workers at the Third Global Forum on Human Resources for Health in Recife, Brazil. At this forum, 57 countries—including Liberia and Guinea—made specific health workforce commitments, for several of which IntraHealth provided technical guidance in crafting. Guinea's commitment focused on its desire to get more frontline health workers to two rural provinces where they were largely absent. One of those regions, N'Zerekore, is the same region where ''patient zero'' of the current Ebola epidemic was believed to be infected—less than a month after Guinea made this commitment. Yet as many African countries stood up to make their commitments clear in Recife, only one donor commitment to health workforce strengthening was made. That financial commitment was made by Ireland.

Let me be clear: because of the generosity of the American people and the know-how and innovations of implementing partners such as IntraHealth, the United States government has made huge inroads in helping countries improve the numbers, the competencies, and the support for health workers in West Africa and around the world.

For example, a major issue Liberia now faces is the need to quickly get the latest information to its health workers. IntraHealth and UNICEF are currently working with the Liberian Government on a tool called mHero to allow the Ministry of Health and health workers to instantly communicate critical information to one another. The USAID-supported, open source, online personnel management system IntraHealth is using for this effort, called iHRIS, has already saved our low-income country partners approximately $232 million in 20 countries around the world—and many of these countries are using iHRIS data to successfully drive more domestic investment in health workers.

In Liberia, more than 8,000 health workers are registered in iHRIS. This open source system will save Liberia more than $3.1 million in proprietary fees over the next 5 years—equivalent to the annual salaries of 317 Liberian nurses for 5 years. These nurses could provide 634,000 Liberians access to lifesaving services.

Innovations such as iHRIS that are supported by American foreign assistance are critical to addressing some specific workforce challenges, but certainly not all of them. I believe if you asked any administration official to articulate the United States strategy or its cumulative results across agencies in assisting partner countries in strengthening their health workforce, they could not tell you.

The Frontline Health Workers Coalition, an alliance of 41 U.S.-based public- and private-sector organizations and of which IntraHealth is proud to host the Secretariat and help lead, last month released recommendations for how the United States can lead in helping the countries of West Africa and other low-income country partners build the resilient and sustainable workforce we need for the 21st century.

I've included our full recommendations as an addendum to my testimony. In brief, there must be a more concerted effort to address the needs of local health workers in Liberia, Sierra Leone, and Guinea. This includes ensuring timely delivery of hazard pay, ensuring an effective and efficient supply chain management system that provides personal protective equipment and other necessary supplies with requisite training, creating supply outposts for local health workers, making psychosocial support available, addressing Ebola-related stigma that has arisen, and increasing the authority of local management of health workers.

This support to local workers—a critical first step to rebuilding the health systems of these countries—must be backed by an equally fervent political push for global action to meaningfully address the most critical deficiencies of the global frontline health workforce. A 2010 IntraHealth report estimated that by 2020, the United States needs to invest at least $5.5 billion in health workforce strengthening to achieve the global health goals and targets to which it has committed.

The robust bipartisan support for global health must also continue to ensure Ebola does not set back the extraordinary progress we've made in the last decade. And I believe each procurement for those investments should be required to show how it will help strengthen health workforces and systems.

U.S. health workforce investments must be guided by a multiyear, costed, cross-agency strategy with an implementation plan that sends an unequivocal message to our developing country partners: that America is committed to this issue and we expect others to respond in kind. This clear sign of commitment would go a long way in helping to ensure a serious and coordinated effort by all governments for a financed global health workforce strategy with specific timelines and targets.

I would like to close by asking each of us to pause and think about what it would be like to wake up tomorrow morning infected with Ebola and not have a single person to turn to for health care. Or to have your infant child this evening show signs of malaria, and have nowhere to take her. This is reality for far too many—and it must be changed now.

Frontline health workers have started to turn the tide on Ebola at great risk to their own lives—WHO reports as of November 30, 622 health workers have been infected during the epidemic, 346 of whom have died. We would be doing a great disservice to health workers' sacrifices if we didn't focus on their immediate needs and at the same time work just as fervently to ensure we never again have a crisis of this scale in public health.

Thank you very much, and I look forward to answering your questions.

ATTACHMENT

INTRAHEALTH INTERNATIONAL—BUILDING A RESILIENT, SUSTAINABLE HEALTH
WORKFORCE TO RESPOND TO EBOLA AND OTHER FUTURE THREATS

FRONTLINE HEALTH WORKERS COALITION POLICY RECOMMENDATIONS—NOVEMBER 2014

The Ebola virus disease epidemic in West Africa has highlighted the urgent need for increased support for frontline health workers and the systems that support them in the region and around the world. The World Health Organization (WHO) reports that as of Nov. 2, 2014, 546 health workers have been infected with Ebola since the onset of the epidemic, and 310 of them have died caring for the more than 13,000 people confirmed or suspected to be infected with the virus.

Nearly all of these lives have been lost in three countries—Guinea, Liberia, and Sierra Leone—that have some of the lowest numbers of health workers per capita in the world. These three countries all had less than three doctors, nurses or midwives per every 10,000 people before the Ebola epidemic even took hold, far less than the 22.8 per 10,000 ratio WHO says is the minimum needed to deliver basic health services.

Access to competent and supported health workers can no longer be allowed to languish as a global health policy afterthought. The heroic sacrifices of frontline health workers must be met with honor, compassion, and support for their efforts. Investments must be made in equipment, supplies, training, effective management and financial support for the retention of health workers to ensure that every community has the workforce needed to save lives, and the robust systems to support those workers in detecting, analyzing and responding to new and emerging public health threats like Ebola.

The Frontline Health Workers Coalition recommends that the U.S. Government and its partners address this public health emergency and help build a sustainable response to future emergencies by taking the following actions:

In Guinea, Liberia, and Sierra Leone

- Increase support for local health workers on the frontlines of the Ebola fight: Working with health ministries, professional associations, local governments and communities, and nongovernmental organizations (NGOs), the U.S. can support local health workers by:
    - Æ Supporting the financing and timely delivery of hazardous duty pay and death and insurance benefits for local health workers during the period of active crisis;
    - Æ Ensuring personal protective equipment (PPE) and infection control supplies are provided to health workers with the requisite training and supervision for safe and consistent use;
    - Æ Ensuring the availability of psychosocial support for health workers and specific treatment units or centers dedicated to health workers who become infected with Ebola;
    - Æ Creating supply outposts for health workers to collect food, clean water and basic supplies;
    - Æ Improving data collection and dissemination efforts about the epidemic, including data on the health workforce, patient tracking and supply chain;
    - Æ Supporting the recruitment of health workers from the region to respond to the epidemic and assist in bringing routine health services back to normal;
    - Æ Increasing capacity and authority for local management of health workers.
- Build a responsive and sustainable supply-chain management system: Health workers' ability to continue fighting Ebola depends on having adequate equipment, supplies, and medicines. The U.S. should work to ensure that both local and international health workers have the supplies they need through a responsive and sustainable supply chain management system.
- Ensure a sustainable frontline health workforce by supporting training programs: The World Bank estimates that at least 5,000 additional health workers are needed to respond to the current epidemic. Maintaining and scaling up educational and training programs, such as medical and nursing schools for new health workers, is critical to building a sustainable response. The U.S. should:
    - Æ Support scale-up of enrollment of students from rural communities into health professional schools and community health worker training programs;
    - Æ Ensure educational programs for health workers are open and adequately staffed and funded to meet local health labor market demand. Liberia's

health professional schools are currently closed, and they must be assisted to reopen;

Æ Ensure all health worker training programs provide adequate infection control information on Ebola and other transmissible agents.

- Address stigma:

    Æ Frontline health workers and their families have been attacked, stigmatized and even thrown out of their homes and communities while risking their lives to care for those infected with Ebola. The U.S. should work with partners to ensure health workers are protected and honored for their work.

    Æ The U.S. should work with partners and communities to leverage media and communications channels to promote messages about protecting health workers as a national and community asset. Community members and health workers should to be encouraged to share their stories to directly address stigma and psychosocial issues.

Worldwide

- Provide new investments that could help:

    Æ Jumpstart U.S. partner country efforts to strengthen their health workforce's capacity to quell Ebola and other public health emergencies as part of the Global Health Security Agenda. The United Nations estimated that it will cost at least $600 million to halt the current Ebola epidemic in West Africa.

    Æ Build a sustainable frontline health workforce in partner countries to achieve the U.S. Government's core global health priorities (ensuring global health security, ending preventable child and maternal deaths, and achieving an AIDS-free generation). A report from FHWC member IntraHealth International estimated that the U.S. should invest at least $5.5 billion by 2020 [1] to help strengthen the health workforce to achieve USG global health goals.

- Ensure through continued robust investments across global health that Ebola does not set back the extraordinary progress of recent decades in saving lives and preventing the spread of diseases.
- Release a multiyear, costed, cross-agency health workforce strategy with an implementation plan that sends an unequivocal message about how the United States will support partner countries to ensure that communities have access to health workers who are supported and equipped to save lives and stop public health threats. This strategy should include concrete targets and benchmarks and have clear mechanisms for monitoring progress.
- Provide specific targets that include key cadres of health workers, necessary financing and an implementation timeline for the following goal of the Global Health Security Agenda:

    Æ "The United States will also support countries in substantially accomplishing: A workforce including physicians, veterinarians, biostatisticians, laboratory scientists, and at least 1 trained field epidemiologist per 200,000 population, who can systematically cooperate to meet relevant IHR and PVS core competencies."

- Advocate strongly for the World Health Organization to adopt at the 2016 World Health Assembly a financed global health workforce strategy that sets specific targets, timelines, and commitments for ensuring that by 2030:

    Æ All communities will have access to competent health workers, trained and supported to save lives and improve health;

    Æ All countries will have the health workforce and systems needed to stop Ebola and other existing and emerging public health threats.

End Note

[1] The IntraHealth International report Saving Lives, Ensuring a Legacy (2010) recommends the U.S. Government invest at least $5.5 billion by 2020 dedicated to strengthening health workforce in partner countries to address severe shortages and human resources for health (HRH) deficiencies in U.S. Government partner countries. As of November 2014, the U.S. Government currently does not have mandated funding allocations for health workforce. A detailed explanation of the methodology used for this estimate is available in the report: http://www.intrahealth.org/files/media/saving-lives-ensuring-a-legacy-a-health-workforce-strategy-for-the-global-health-initiative/IntraHealthlPolicylPaperl1.pdf.

Senator COONS. Thank you, Mr. Gaye.

Mr. Alvarez.

STATEMENT OF JAVIER ALVAREZ, SENIOR TEAM LEAD, STRATEGIC RESPONSE AND GLOBAL EMERGENCIES, MERCY CORPS, PORTLAND, OR

Mr. ALVAREZ. Mr. Chairman Coons, Ranking Member Flake, and members of the committee, Your Excellency President, I would like to take the opportunity again to meet you. We met a couple of weeks ago in a social mobilization subcommittee, another subcommittee, and thank you very much for the support you are giving to the entire humanitarian community but also to Mercy Corps.

Thank you for inviting me to testify today on this critical crisis. I speak today in my capacity as senior team leader of the Strategic Response and Global Emergencies Team for Mercy Corps, a global humanitarian and development organization. I have just returned from Liberia, where I served as Country Director for Mercy Corps Liberia.

Mercy Corps has worked in Liberia since 2002, supporting its transition from civil war to sustainable economic and social development. While our core programs focus on reviving agricultural markets, job creation, and youth entrepreneurship, our Ebola response has focused on two pillars: reducing transmission through community education and mobilization campaigns, and to mitigate the socioeconomic impacts of the crisis on Liberian communities and the region.

For the purpose of this hearing, I would like to focus on the second pillar, as my colleagues have covered already most of the health crisis.

The Ebola outbreak has been largely approached as a health crisis. I am very glad to hear Madam President's announcement today of the launch of the possible comprehensive plan, economic plan. From Mercy Corps' perspective it is better understood as a system crisis, the failure of health governance humanitarian systems to prevent a disease from disrupting the socioeconomic order of communities and countries.

Adopting a systems approach to the planning, management, and monetary needs are therefore critical, and the recovery efforts must right-size emergency efforts and work toward long-term development goals so that future shocks are not as disastrously disruptive.

In October, Mercy Corps conducted an economic assessment to better understand the economic impacts of the crisis in people's daily lives. We found three major findings now guiding our response.

First, household incomes, food security, and food consumption have been greatly reduced by the Ebola crisis. Without targeted interventions and policy changes now, households could face a critical level of food insecurity by April–May 2015.

Second, some of the protocols and policies associated with the Ebola crisis have put significant strain on the Liberian economy.

And third, disproportionate economic impacts are being felt by youth, self-employed persons, and lower-wage workers. This threatens the stability of Liberia and the region.

Food insecurity in Liberia was already widespread before the Ebola crisis, with 42 percent of the population considered food insecure and 32 percent of children stunted. As a result of the crisis, vulnerable households are reducing food consumed at each meal, purchasing lower quality meals or less expensive food, and eating fewer meals. At the same time, some of the protocols deemed necessary for Ebola containment are creating constraints and blockages in the market system. These include border closures, market closures, and increased transportation costs and time.

In August, the Government of Liberia closed borders with Guinea, Sierra Leone and Ivory Coast, imposed a 12 a.m. to 6 a.m. curfew, and recommended the closure of weekly markets. Goods that were previously sourced quickly and cheaply from Guinea and the Ivory Coast are no longer available. Traders cannot afford to move goods from Monrovia to northern markets due to increased costs, and a lot of agricultural goods spoil before reaching their destination due to the curfew.

Traders currently cannot keep markets alive. Further compounding these economic stressors is the uncertainty of Liberian agriculture. Fortunately, weekly markets have been now reopened. This is welcome news. However, policies restricting movement are still putting downward pressure on the volume of goods moving between markets and households.

Finally, the impacts of the Ebola crisis have had a disproportionate impact on low-wage workers and the self-employed, who are mainly urban youth. Seventy percent of Liberia's population is under 35. Productive engagement of youth was a major priority and challenge before the crisis and will now be more difficult. It is thus critical that youth are at the center of early recovery planning, implementation and management, ensuring they gain the skills, opportunities and experience they need to become active drivers of Liberia's economy.

There are several short- and medium-term actions that can be taken to support markets, prevent a food security crisis, and lay the foundations for early recovery. Within the United States, we thank you for robustly funding the Ebola supplement and the International Disaster Assistance Account in the fiscal year 2015 appropriations process. As you know, the humanitarian system is under extraordinary stress in the face of Ebola, Syria, Iraq, South Sudan, and the Central African Republic.

We further urge that the administration should target short-term food security and income recovery interventions toward the worst affected communities, with the goal of increasing access to income through well-targeted cash programming with careful market monitoring.

All relevant government entities plan and budget for a pro-poor, market-based early recovery strategy in Liberia in the region now. Strategies should seek to address the root causes of chronic underdevelopment.

In Monrovia, changes to government-imposed regulations, so long deemed appropriate from a public health standpoint, could decrease economic stress. This includes opening the borders or negotiating an economic corridor to allow essential goods to cross from neighboring countries, addressing constraints that policies are imposing on trade. Issuing permits allowing commercial vehicles to travel during curfew hours and pass more easily through checkpoints is one idea.

Among donors and implementing partners, we recommend monitoring markets, prices, and systems constraints by investing financial resources and human capital in assessments; invest in learning and capacity-building; preventing regional economic decline by embedding market conflict and political economic analysts in regional responsive sectors; and ensuring close coordination between financial institutions, governments, NGOs, and civil society.

Again, I wish to sincerely thank the subcommittee, and Your Excellency as well, for your leadership on this critical crisis, and the great honor of extending me the privilege of testifying today. I look forward to your questions.

Thank you.

[The prepared statement of Mr. Alvarez follows:]

PREPARED STATEMENT OF JAVIER ALVAREZ

Chairman Coons, Ranking Member Flake and members of the committee, thank you for inviting me to testify before this esteemed subcommittee on the critical issue of ensuring a sustained and strategic international response to the Ebola crisis. I speak today in my capacity as Senior Team Lead of the Strategic Response and Global Emergencies unit for Mercy Corps, a global humanitarian and development organization saving and improving lives in the world's toughest places. With a network of experienced professionals in more than 40 crisis-affected countries worldwide, Mercy Corps partners with local communities to help people recover, overcome hardship and build resilience to future shocks.

Mercy Corps has worked in Liberia since 2002, supporting its transition from civil war to sustainable economic and social development. Our programs focus on reviving agricultural markets and creating jobs, with a particular focus on youth entrepreneurship and leadership and access to financial services. Our Ebola response has focused on two pillars based on close monitoring and assessment of gaps in the response: (1) filling a gap in community education on how to reduce transmission by mobilizing a robust social mobilization campaign, and (2) mitigating the socioeconomic impacts of the crisis on Liberian communities, and the region. For the purposes of this hearing, I will focus on the second pillar.

I have just returned from 2 months in Liberia where I served as Acting Country Director for Mercy Corps Liberia. My testimony will outline how Mercy Corps sees the crisis, highlight findings from our market assessment and gaps we see in the current response, and will conclude by suggesting a series of short- and medium-term solutions to ensure a successful international response.

MORE THAN A HEALTH CRISIS, A SYSTEMS CRISIS

As my copanelists have detailed, Ebola has wreaked havoc across five West African nations since the outbreak began in February 2014. Liberia is the nation most severely affected by the crisis, suffering almost half of all cumulative confirmed, probable and suspected cases reported (7,690), with 3,161 deaths as of December 8,
Having originally arrived through the porous border with neighboring Guinea, it has spread from the rural Lofa County to reach every one of Liberia's 15 counties including the capital city, Monrovia. This has created the most serious Ebola epidemic in history, which not only directly threatens the lives of tens of thousands of people, but jeopardizes the economic progress and stability Liberia has achieved since a protracted civil war ended a decade ago.

The Ebola outbreak has been approached largely as a health crisis. From Mercy Corps' perspective, it is better understood as a systems crisis—the failure of health, governance, and humanitarian systems to mitigate the threat of a disease from disrupting the socioeconomic order of communities and multiple countries. And the longer the crisis continues, the greater potential it has to contribute to another systems failure—a failure of market systems.

Fortunately, Liberians and all West Africans have shown extraordinary resilience and ingenuity in the face of this crisis, transmission rates have started to slow and some market activities have resumed. However, this is no means for pause. The Ebola epidemic continues to cripple the economies of Liberia, Sierra Leone, and Guinea; has left thousands of civilians unemployed and hundreds of thousands of households more vulnerable to food insecurity; and the social fabric of an already fragile nation—just before a tenuous election season—has been further eroded.

Adopting a systems approach to the planning, management, and monitoring of this crisis—by broadening the set of analytical tools, planning strategies, and funding streams to address it—is critical to ensuring a successful crisis response and building more inclusive, responsive, and resilient communities and institutions along the way.

MAJOR SOCIOECONOMIC IMPACTS OF THE EBOLA CRISIS

To better understand the socioeconomic impacts of the Ebola crisis on households, vendors and markets in Liberia, Mercy Corps conducted an economic assessment in Lofa and Nimba counties and in parts of the capital, Monrovia, from Oct. 3–13, 2014. Findings from the assessment and our ongoing programs in Liberia point us to three major areas of focus for the response, and my testimony, moving forward:

1. Household incomes, food security, and food consumption have been greatly reduced by the Ebola crisis. Without targeted interventions and policy changes now, households could face a critical level of food insecurity by April/May of 2015;

2. Some of the protocols and policies associated with the Ebola crisis have put a significant strain on the Liberian economy; and

3. Disproportionate economic impacts are being felt by youth, self-employed persons, and lower wage workers. This threatens Liberia's, and the region's, stability.

1. Risk of a food security crisis by April/May 2015

Food insecurity in Liberia was already widespread before the Ebola crisis, with 42 percent of the population considered food insecure, and 32 percent of children classified as stunted.[2] Still fighting to recover from years of civil war, Liberia continues to be one of the world's poorest countries, ranked 162 out of 169 countries in the 2010 United Nations Development Program (UNDP) Human Development Index, with up to 84 percent of its population live below the national poverty line, on less than $1.25 day.[3]

As a result of both the Ebola crisis and precrisis economic inequalities, vulnerable households started reducing the amount of food consumed at each meal (mentioned by over 90 percent of households interviewed in our assessment), purchasing lower quality or less expensive food, and eating fewer meals (mentioned by 90 percent and 85 percent respectively). Seventy-seven percent of those interviewed cited borrowing money from friends and relatives as an additional coping mechanism. Households in general are spending most of their income on food products. These coping mechanisms could have lasting negative impacts on people's nutritional status and economic investments and may jeopardize their future ability to recover.

Constraints on household food security caused by reduced incomes and increased prices may also be compounded by uncertain agricultural yields from the next harvest. Upland and lowland rice harvests in October/November and January/February may provide temporary relief for agricultural households in Lofa and Nimba counties, but it remains unclear. If the overall situation continues without changes and if the economy experiences production decreases, food insecurity would increase significantly by April/May 2015.

2. Constraints in the market system imposed by the Ebola response

Some of the protocols deemed necessary for Ebola containment are creating additional constraints and blockages in the market system, namely:

- Border closures,
- Closure of markets, and
- Spiked transport costs and increased transportation time due to the 12 a.m.-6 a.m. curfew, checkpoints, and other regulations.

Regarding border closures, the Government of Liberia closed borders with Guinea, Sierra Leone, and Ivory Coast and at the same time recommended the closure of weekly markets as Ebola prevention measures in August 2014. As a result, goods that were previously sourced quickly and cheaply from Guinea and Ivory Coast are no longer available due to border closures, causing vendors to source replacement goods at higher prices with longer transportation times.

One vendor we spoke with previously spent 2,000LD on a trip to Guinea to purchase goods for her shop. Now with borders closed, she must travel further to Monrovia to purchase goods and the trip costs her 5,000LD. She passes this cost increase along to her customers through increased prices at her shop in the market.

Weekly market days have been reopened to allow for increased trade between counties. This is great news. However, policies restricting internal movement are still puting downward pressure on the volume of goods moving between markets and households.

The impact of Ebola policies on transport prices has also been significant. Border closures and reduced consumer demand have contributed to an increase in transport costs and a reduction in the number of vehicles transporting goods. Checkpoints and regulations limiting the number of passengers in vehicles, the inability of vehicles to travel during curfew hours, and delays due to road blocks have also contributed to the increase in transportation prices. A rapid assessment of the transportation market is needed to help inform a short- and medium-term program to increase access to transportation for economic purposes. A more robust transportation system can reduce market costs for consumers, including for food items, increasing households' food security.

3. Disproportionate economic impacts on workers and self-employed, including youth

The economic impacts of the Ebola crisis have had a particular impact on workers and those who are self-employed—particularly youth in urban areas. A cell phone survey commissioned by the World Bank throughout October and November indicates generally lower incomes and jobs being shed in both the wage-earning and the self-employed sectors—sectors largely composed of youth.[4]

Liberian youth, defined as 15–35-year-olds, represent a third of the country's population, with 70 percent of its total population under 35. Productive engagement of youth a priority and major challenge for economic development efforts even before the crisis, as social ties between youth and their communities were severely damaged by the country's long civil war, the resulting displacement, and rural-to-urban migration making.

Many of these youth have been frustrated by the international community's post-conflict response to Liberia for over a decade, feeling that their opinions have marginalized from planning processes and their capacities for productive engagement in society disregarded. In this capacity, youth are key to reducing risks of future instability in Liberia.

It is thus critical that youth are at the center of early recovery planning, implementation and management, ensuring they gain the skills, opportunities and experience they need to become active drivers of Liberia's economy.

RECOMMENDATIONS FOR IMMEDIATE AND FUTURE ACTION

There are several short- and medium-term actions that can be taken in the U.S., in Monrovia, and within the humanitarian response to mitigate the cascading socio-economic impacts of the crisis on households and the region, prevent a food security crisis in April/May 2015 and lay the foundations for early recovery.

Within the U.S., we recommend that:

1. Congress robustly fund the International Disaster Assistance Account in the FY15 appropriations process at $3.5 billion given the extraordinary demands on the global humanitarian system in the face of Ebola, Syria, Iraq, South Sudan, and the Central African Republic. As you surely know, the United Nations appealed Monday for a record $16.4 billion global appeal in order to address unprecedented global humanitarian needs in 2015.

2. The administration should target short-term food security and income recovery interventions toward the worst affected communities, with the goal of increasing access to income through well-targeted cash programming with careful market monitoring to ensure food supplies are available.

3. All relevant government entities should simultaneously and jointly plan and budget for a pro-poor market-based early recovery strategy in Liberia that addresses the root causes of underdevelopment. U.S. strategies should be aligned with those of Liberian youth and civil society, the Government of Liberia, U.N., World Bank, and other major actors, and must seek to lay the foundations for an economic recovery agenda that addresses the root causes of economic inequality, stagnation and chronic underdevelopment.

In Monrovia, changes to government-imposed regulations, so long as deemed appropriate from a public health standpoint, could lessen the spikes in transportation costs that are reducing economic activity and increasing household vulnerability. These include:

1. Open the borders or negotiate an economic corridor to allow essential goods to cross from neighboring countries by traders screened at the border.

2. Address constraints that the curfew is imposing on trade. Issuing permit to commercial vehicles to travel during curfew hours and facilitate their passage at checkpoints could immediately address some of the time burdens that traders currently face.

Within the donor and implementing partner community:

1. Monitor markets, prices and systems constraints iteratively by investing financial resources and human capital in sustained multisector assessments. Pay close attention to any shortages or adverse economic effects and take corrective actions, as necessary.

2. Invest in learning and capacity-building throughout the response. We have a responsibility to learn from this crisis, capture and utilize transferable knowledge, and support local leadership of Liberians at every level of the response.

For example, Mercy Corps' current USAID-funded social mobilization Ebola prevention program, the Ebola Community Action Platform, has a major learning component focused on real-time information gathering to understand how communities respond to information in this crisis, to inform feedback on immediate improvements to programming and lessons for strategic planning to disaster risk reduction and crisis prevention in the future. While I did not focus on this program during my testimony, I am happy to discuss it in Q&A.

3. Stay ahead of the potential for regional economic decline by embedding market, conflict and political economy analysts in the UNMEER structure, and ensuring close coordination between financial institutions such as the World Bank and African Development Bank, government actors and NGOs.

Again, I wish to sincerely thank the subcommittee for its leadership on this critical crisis, and the great honor of extending me the privilege of testifying today. I look forward to answering any questions.

End Notes

[1] http://www.cdc.gov/vhf/ebola/outbreaks/2014-west-africa/case-counts.html.

[2] DHS , Republic of Liberia—2013.

[3] World Bank, Liberia—poverty headcount ratio. http://data.worldbank.org/Country/Liberia.

[4] World Bank, Update on the Economic Impact of the 2014 Ebola Epidemic on Liberia, Sierra Leone, and Guinea, December 2, 2014. http://www.worldbank.org/en/topic/growth/publication/economic-update-ebola-december.

Senator COONS. Thank you very much, Mr. Alvarez.

I would like to thank the entire panel.

We have a relatively brief period, so I will have us go to 5-minute rounds, and I am just going to ask one question of each of the four of you. If I could ask for a relatively concise answer, that will allow my colleagues a chance to question as well.

You have said, Dr. Farmer, this is a caretaker disease in the context of very weak health systems. I will carry the phrase ''zoonoses'' with me from this hearing, something I will drop casually in social settings in Delaware and impress people with my great knowledge of zoonoses, something I was previously unfamiliar with.

The challenge of having a clear term for what it means to do public health systems strengthening I think can best be summarized this way. As Senator Durbin said to me, when we roll up a major intervention that includes DOD and the Public Health Service and then leave, sometimes we look at what are we leaving behind. And I hope we would instead look at what are we doing to build health forward.

What are we doing, as you put it, Dr. Peterson, to invest in building sustainably? Are we, as we respond to this emergency, building sustainable public health systems for Liberia, Sierra Leone, Guinea, and the region?

So, Dr. Farmer, my question for you: What is the one thing in your view that we would do that would most contribute to building forward a meaningful public health system?

To Dr. Peterson, one of your points was that we need to more effectively listen to the faith community on the ground. What is the number one thing you would urge us to do to incorporate that into our responses?

To Mr. Gaye, how do we engage the African diaspora better and mobilize the resources that the President referred to of the many doctors and health care workers who have fled the region during conflict and could possibly be returned back? And how does health worker safety play into that?

And if we have any time left, Mr. Alvarez, what role does stigma play in the economic impact? My concern is that the regional economies, as you pointed out in great detail, are heading south rapidly, and if we do not open borders and reduce stigma, we will not return to economic growth and thus real recovery from this Ebola outbreak.

Thank you to all four witnesses. I would urge you to endeavor to give brief replies.

Dr. FARMER. Concision is not my strong suit, Senator, but I will skip ahead from the obvious point that we need these four S's: staff, stuff, space, and systems. It is a point that has been made by the President, by everyone here.

I think, to take a critical look at the legacy of our investments, we should just use some examples. When we say we need to build local capacity, that term can be distorted and perverted in many ways. It could end up meaning, as it often does, 2-day workshops on infection control, say, or clinical management of Ebola. That is not really what our colleagues and partners need.

They need the same things that we have, formal credentialed training programs in medicine, in nursing, in public health, and in health care management. Those take years to build. That is why I think the President mentioned the Human Resources for Health program that the Clinton Foundation had been working on with the Ministry of Health for many months before the crisis. That is a program that deserves to be supported, and it is what our partners are asking for.

So the differences between a workshop, fine, but not what we need, which is long-term training programs. It took me 8 years to train as an infectious disease doctor. It takes a surgeon even more. And there is so much human capital in this part of the world, there is so much talent. Give them a chance to have formal training.

The second point I will just pass on is look at the infrastructure that we are building. I actually had a picture—I am sorry I do not know how to resurrect it on the screen—comparing an Ebola treatment unit that I saw in rural Liberia with the hospital that we built in rural Haiti, also an unelectrified region. It is the largest solar-powered hospital in the developing world today. It is the largest training center for Haitian doctors and nurses. It is the kind of investment that we need to link to our emergency response in West Africa.

Thank you.

Senator COONS. Thank you, Dr. Farmer, and thank you for being with us.

Dr. Peterson.

Dr. PETERSON. Thank you for your question. I think that the best way to explain how we can listen better to communities and link to faith-based organizations is to talk about some of the things that are actually happening and happening well in Sierra Leone, and I saw it more in Sierra Leone than in Liberia.

World Vision is leading a number of coalitions. The coalitions include Christians, Catholics, and Muslims together. One coalition is pulling together burials, safe and dignified burials in 12 of the 14 districts, allowing families to have someone to pray for their loved ones, to meet the cultural traditions. They are also trusted by the donor, in this case DFID, because the Ministry of Health money did not actually pay the burial teams, but World Vision as an organization that knows how to do fiscal management can manage logistics, can do fiscal management, and is beginning to do that very critical service to the community in a way that both meets donor needs and meets the people's cultural needs.

Similarly, there is another coalition, again Muslim and Christian and Catholic, that is looking at what are the important messages that the community needs to hear, what are their fears, how do we frame the science that we have from CDC and NIH in a way that it is understandable in a faith language. They are putting together training for faith leaders—Muslim, Christian, pastors, priests—and beginning to reach through that whole network of faith leaders into the communities, which will begin to transform behavior. I think that is how we can do it.

Thank you.

Senator COONS. Thank you.

Mr. Gaye, briefly.

Mr. GAYE. Yes. Thank you for the question on how to better engage African diaspora. There is a lot of talent sitting in this country, and in these phases of crisis there are a lot of people who want to help.

I think there are only two very simple things we need to do, and they are both about information. A lot of people want to help. They do not know where to go. If we manage to create good information flows and collect a repository of groups that are doing this, I think that we will go a long way.

The second thing we need to do is to build on the platforms that already exist. There are some very good examples of practices that I would certainly encourage. The Global Health Corps is one of these. I think the young Barbara Bush is leading that. It is very clever in pairing up young American and young foreigners to engage in an internship. In fact, IntraHealth is hosting two of them. They might even be in the room. So programs like that need to be replicated because I think they expand the idea that you could serve Africa by being here.

Then we can look into examples in the private sector. Pfizer, for example, has a great global health program where they encourage their employees to go overseas. For the majority of companies that have these programs, it would be fantastic for the diaspora that works with these companies to know these programs exist. So I think we need to publicize more of this.

It is all about information and providing the right information.

Senator COONS. Thank you, Mr. Gaye.

Mr. Alvarez, in one sentence, how do we deal with economic stigma?

Mr. ALVAREZ. So, yes, I think it is part of an equation. The stigma of the survivors returning back to their communities is becoming a huge issue, as the representative already mentioned. There are more and more survivors. So the ones that want to come back are sometimes ostracized and sidelined. So those people, if we see them as engines of change in the economic recovery, we are losing a huge opportunity.

Again, it all comes down to information, misinformation, community involvement. And, of course, you know, the movement of goods has been reduced, and we see that as affecting the livelihoods of households. There will be more food insecurity.

So stigma is going to become the next big issue. Messaging so far has been focusing on "Ebola Kills," "Ebola is Real." It has been more promoting the negative. Now we are at a juncture that that messaging needs to change, and we have to offer people the hope and the forward looking that we are seeing from the fears.

Thank you, Mr. Chairman.

Senator COONS. Thank you, and I would like to thank our whole panel.

Senator Flake.

Senator FLAKE. Thank you.

I appreciate the testimony, and I know it must be intimidating speaking with the President of Liberia literally looking over your shoulder here. [Laughter.]

It speaks well for her that she wants to hear what is going on here.

I just have one, in my limited time here, one question that I hope all of you can address very briefly, and I hope that we can follow up with you.

We have a phenomenon here often when we fund operations overseas—just take Afghanistan, for example. We are finding many examples now of appropriating a lot of money that builds a facility that was right and proper for an occupying force but does not serve those who are left behind. We have talked with some of you saying we need to address the concerns of health workers that will be there afterward, after the expats leave.

What would you caution us in terms of how we appropriate, and procurement rules, and whatever we have to deal with here to make sure that we can respond nimbly to the changes that are being made? I would think that we may not have thought a couple of months ago that Liberia would be in the situation that they are right now with just 10 new cases per day. We want to make sure that the funding we provide, the resources we provide are addressing the needs now and in the future rather than addressing needs in the past. The last thing we want are facilities that we built that were fine for a lot of expats there or the response that we have had in the past rather than public health centers that we need in the future.

What cautions would you give us or what advice in terms of our role here in terms of oversight now that can help for the long term?

Dr. Farmer, any thoughts?

Dr. FARMER. Thank you very much, Senator. That is a terrific question, and I think if I were to signal the biggest trap I think for us—for you and for us—is the trap of double standards, which is very common, I fear, in development work in public health, international health.

Example: If we build a facility, one of the things that we should be pushing for as a metric is very low case fatality rates. So, in other words, people who are diagnosed with Ebola, what is the harm of saying, as people who are supporting this, we want to see less than 10 percent die? We want 90 percent survival rate. What is the harm of that? There is no harm.

No American has died from Ebola because when they get into the embrace of our—granted—dysfunctional health care system, they get good critical care, and you cannot take care of people with Ebola who are losing up to 10 liters of fluid a day from vomiting and diarrhea without good medical care, with an intravenous line and a nurse or a physician administering it.

So I think we should reject the double standards. What is appropriate for the physiology of a Liberian or a Sierra Leonean or a Guinean with Ebola is the same as what is appropriate for us. It is just that they do not have the systems, and we should help them build them.

I think the other big trap is related; the trap of the contractual, the trap of thinking there is a beginning and an end to this accompaniment process. This is going to be a long term. We are making significant investments in West Africa. We should be thinking long term, just as the President said. We have to link our emergency response to rebuilding systems, and that is going to take a long time.

Senator FLAKE. Thank you.

Dr. FARMER. Thank you, sir.

Senator FLAKE. Dr. Peterson, briefly.

Dr. PETERSON. Yes, thank you. I spent a lot of time in Afghanistan, so I actually really appreciate that question. The rebuilding of the health system within Afghanistan, I think, is very appropriate for this issue because, in fact, they did it fairly systematically.

I will also repeat my earlier comment that listening is very helpful. The Minister of Health of Afghanistan said no-thank-you to a great big clinic hospital in the center of Kabul. What she wanted for her country were rural centers, training of midwives and community health workers. And that, in fact, built the long-term sustainability.

The other thing that Afghanistan did that I think would make a difference in this Ebola response is they focused on management training for the health system, for the provincial and medical and district directors. How do they actually do fiscal accountability? How do they do supply logistics? Some of our NGOs provided that kind of expertise for health systems management, and I think that was really key.

The other piece in the management rebuilding that helped there and could make a big difference in Africa is the whole health management information system, another not very sexy acronym, but set up data that provided transparency so that it was harder for money to go astray and easier to know whether you were truly making the difference in improving the health system.

If we took some of those experiences that worked well in Afghanistan, not everything worked well, but those things that did work well and applied it to rebuilding the health system in the West African context, I think we would do better.

Thank you.

Senator FLAKE. Well, thank you.

My time is up. But if you can briefly, very briefly, respond?

Mr. GAYE. So, just a couple of points. One: is it is a different type of mind-set to get into building these systems because it does take a little longer. I know that the issue of the health workforce is not new. Senator Durbin, I know for a fact that in 2008 you supported legislation to support the health workforce. So that is the first mind-shift we need to make.

Second, we do need to have a good strategy to guide this investment, a strategy that is going to do one thing, make sure that at the country level we have checks and balances. The way you are going to do this is by investing more with civil society. There are a lot more actors in the countries that are ready to jump in, and we just need to create a safe space and a good space for them to engage and support the government work.

Mr. ALVAREZ. Thank you. Just one very quick point. I think one of the more intelligent approaches to funding of partners in Liberia, agencies like Mercy Corps, we would like to see very flexible approaches to funding. I mean, the situation is evolving. There are a lot of moving pieces. So moving from an emergency standpoint that we are close to coming to an early economic development phase that will allow us to be able to be responding to the reality on the ground.

I think another very important piece of advice, very humble advice to give the committee, would be that partners have continuity on the ground. When we saw that the outbreak was there, a lot of partners left the country. I mean, agencies like Mercy Corps and other agencies stayed put, and we have to stay put. There was a fear of the unknown, but we stayed put, and we continue doing our business.

So I think that will be another piece of advice. Thank you.

Senator COONS. Thank you, Senator Flake.

Senator Durbin.

Senator DURBIN. Let me address—and I invite President Sirleaf. Perhaps she can join in responding. Let me address the economics that I found in some parts of Africa. I do not know West Africa as well. Here is what I found when it came to the health care staff and people engaged in this field.

I found that there was a limited capacity for training and education. There was a long-term commitment necessary so that they would develop the skills and training necessary to become doctors, nurses, even health care workers. There was a limited capacity in terms of what training was available, teaching was available, colleges were available.

I found that those that did graduate many times became employees not in the private sector but in the public sector, working for the government of their countries.

I found that they were paid, by Western standards, a very small amount of money each month, and that many times went unpaid for months when the countries would get into budgetary problems.

I found that these skilled health workers, whether they are doctors or nurses in particular, were often poached by England, Europe, and the United States, which could offer them multiples of their promised salaries in Africa, and they took the invitation and left.

How do we stop that from happening? We are talking about an investment here in a bill we are about to vote on of $5.4 billion, according to the Chair, into these countries. I would imagine whether it is Liberia, Sierra Leone, or Guinea, that this is a dramatic increase over the usual public health budget in each country. This is going to fall like manna from the heavens, and the question is how do we translate that into long-term growth of the workers, the health workers that create public health systems, when there is always the lure of leaving and making a lot more money?

Dr. FARMER. Well, I am sure the President has something to say on this. She comes to mind in the exchange we had, Senator. As you all know, the nursing and medical schools are closed in the course of the epidemic. So the training is not happening.

Going back to this experience in Rwanda with the Human Resources for Health program that we have been proposing through the Clinton Foundation and working with our Liberian colleagues, but also in Haiti, to say when have we succeeded in stopping the brain drain? Is it by limiting the free movement of the professionals? No. It is by drawing them back into better health care systems, including public systems. If I were to name a third trap, in response to Senator Flake, it is that if we avoid the public sector, that will be a mistake, the Liberian institutions for example, or Sierra Leonean institutions.

The hospital I mentioned in rural Haiti may have been built by Partners in Health, but it was built by Partners in Health with people from your city, in fact, as you know, very rapidly, 18 months after the earthquake, as a public facility, a teaching facility, and that is why the head of surgery came back after 20 years at Harlem Hospital. That is why the head of medicine came back, Haitian, 15 years in France. That is why the chief of nursing, raised in the United States but a Haitian-American, is there. They have good facilities, and that is a metric we can use if we are putting in billions of dollars.

Senator DURBIN. Can I invite President Sirleaf? Could you address how much is a doctor or nurse or health care worker paid in Liberia, and can you put it in the context of the average wage and whether they are above that?

President SIRLEAF. Let me say that I was a little bit disappointed in ourselves that we were not paying our doctors as much as they should get. Yes, they get much of what the average wage is, but they do get less than, say, some of our high-level officials, and that is something that we are going to correct. Doctors were getting anywhere between $1,500 and $3,000 U.S. dollars, and we do have certain high-level officials that get well over that, somewhere between $5,000 and $6,000. So we are going to have a policy decision that says that they are going to earn as much as our highest officials earn because they make a great investment to get to where they are, and they certainly give great service to our country. So that is going to be corrected.

Senator DURBIN. Thank you.

President SIRLEAF. I do agree generally with all the testimony that has been made, and I would just like to make three quick points.

First, our plan is an evolving one. It is an evolving one that makes the transition from containing Ebola to improving our health care systems to going on to economic recovery. And that evolving plan will ensure that we will have permanence in trying to ensure that we are able to respond to any such breakdown, whether it is through Ebola or a recurrence, or whether it is through other types of diseases.

It will also enable us to have personal capacity through increased per capita incomes that will enable people to live better and to respond to their own health needs in a much more effective way on a personal basis.

The second thing is capacity. I could not agree more with Dr. Farmer that capacity is the key. In our 10-year plan for improving the health care workforce is to build that capacity at all levels, particularly at the bottom—it is like a pyramid—training over 30,000 health care workers at the community level to provide basic health services, and then moving on up to ensure that we then have the physician assistants, the midwives, the nurses, and then finally at the apex, the doctors who are very specialized. So we want to see that plan implemented. It is a long-term plan, but we want to get it started, and we want to make enough progress within the next 2 to 3 years.

Finally, the involvement of the communities. Our success in Ebola has been the active participation and ownership of our communities. As long as we got them involved where they took responsibility to go there and find the sick, to call and have them taken to treatment centers, to be able to respond to those quarantined in the communities, to work with us, we began to get success. So we are going to, in this final push, make sure that the community workers take the lead role and we provide them with the support they need for us to get this job done.

Thank you again for this great hearing.

Senator COONS. Thank you, Madam President. Thank you for your remarks today.

Senator Shaheen.

Senator SHAHEEN. Thank you. I do not have anyone in particular to direct my question to, but as we look at the outbreak in Mali and the potential for other countries, neighboring countries in Africa to be affected, how concerned should we be about that? What kind of lessons have we learned that will help us address those outbreaks, and why was Nigeria able to respond so quickly and address the outbreak there?

And finally, are there any lessons from our involvement with the AIDS virus and the PEPFAR program that should have translated here or that we should be looking at as we think about the current outbreak of Ebola?

Whoever wants to take it.

Dr. FARMER. We are dying to take it.

Dr. PETERSON. All of us. [Laughter.]

I do not think I can speak for Nigeria except it certainly had a more intact health system, which helped enormously. For Mali and the other countries where the health system is weak, it is a danger. One of the things that I think we could do much more quickly and much better is take what we have learned in Liberia and Sierra Leone and bring it there.

I went from Liberia for 10 days and then to Sierra Leone, and both countries were frantically working on their burial protocols and their case management protocols and their logistics protocols, and they were both doing it at the same time. Well, we now have them, both countries have them. We could take that learning and bring it to those countries.

Senator SHAHEEN. Could I just interrupt for a minute? I apologize, but when you say "we," who are we talking about as "we"? Is this something that we are hopeful that all of the organizations that have been working in the currently affected countries will do? Is this something that the U.N. mission should do? Is this something that the United States, that all of us—who is the "we"?

Dr. PETERSON. A brilliant question, because in each of these places it is the combination of the aid agencies and the local governments that are heading every single one of these committees, pillars, et cetera. I found that there was not any communication going on between Sierra Leone and Liberia. In fact, because I had sat in both of those meetings and I was on their email list, I started getting all of the case management protocols from Liberia and said could I send these to Sierra Leone, and I was a complete outsider.

So this is that cross-cutting collaboration. If there was somebody who would take that broad view and say here are all the things that we have learned—maybe it is UNMEER—and bring it to the next country so that they do not have to go through, actually which was what was several months of very good and very hard work, in order to do that collaboration.

As far as learning from the AIDS, I will give an example again from the faith community. World Vision had put together a platform they called Channels of Hope for HIV/AIDS. It was designed to train pastors, imams, other clerics in that sensitive HIV issue, how do we talk to these faith leaders about AIDS and sex, and how do they talk to their congregations. World Vision is using that very same platform for training on Ebola to imams, priests, and others. So those are the kinds of uses of AIDS platforms that I see going on that we should continue.

Thank you.

Dr. FARMER. Can I just say, Senator, that this is the pertinent question in global health, because prior to PEPFAR, there were no major huge programs in global health. They were post-colonial projects. They were public sector engagement inside one's own country. So this was the big game changer.

There is kind of an ugly secret that preceded it that is worth remembering, in the spirit of your question, and that is socialized for scarcity. What our colleagues, what we did in public health was to pit prevention against care.

Of course, that is why the epidemic continued unfettered, because these arguments about managing scarce resources, they really lacked any kind of intellectual depth. They were really all just about funding and scarcity.

What turned that around and made this a success story, especially in the most heavily affected areas? Easing the scarcity with substantial investment, of the level you are talking about for Ebola, and then integrating prevention and care. Then guess what happened? People who were told—and this point was made already by the President and by several of us. If you are told that you are going to die if you get Ebola, then why not stay home? But if you are told we can help you, we can take care of you, we can help you survive, we can make sure you get treatment, people come in for screening, and then we can find out who does not have Ebola and get them treated for malaria or whatever else, or get them back on therapy, including treatment for AIDS. But we need to avoid, this time around, that debate, pitting prevention against care.

Senator SHAHEEN. Thank you.

Mr. Gaye.

Mr. GAYE. Yes, a couple of quick points on lessons from HIV/AIDS. Of course, we see great results when there is rapid mobilization and engagement of everybody that needs to be engaged. We saw the tremendous impact of engaging religious leaders in the HIV/AIDS fight. So with Ebola we have a lot of similarities with stigma and rumors and so forth. So, I think that we can apply these lessons immediately.

On the question of should we worry: yes, we should worry, because the health systems of these countries are extremely weak. This is the time when you say I wish we had invested more in frontline health workers and health workers that were closer to their communities, because in the end they are the ones who are delivering the services. They are the ones. I mean, we have seen it. Study after study has shown that we can reduce these people leaving if we recruit at the community level, at the local level, because when people are recruited and trained where they are from, they tend to go back, and they tend to stay there.

So those are some of the things that I think we could do.

Senator SHAHEEN. Thank you.

Mr. Alvarez.

Mr. ALVAREZ. Thank you very much. So, what I saw there when I was in Liberia was that the numbers started to go down and there was a trend identified that was stable between 10 and 20 cases that the person had mentioned, and in my view it has been a lot about information. The system, the health system has been able to produce detailed information, where these contacts were, which countries, what contact tracing they had, and that information has been able to feed back into the response and be able to track down the disease.

So it has been a reverse trend. Whereas before the disease was hunting us, now the Liberian Government and other health authorities are hunting the disease because they know where they are.

So, how worried should we be about all of this? Very worried. But we think that closing down the borders, if we have that information, should not be one of the measures, or at least the borders are porous anyway, so we should be able to let people cross. I mean, in the north, food insecurity is becoming a big, big issue. Markets are closed. There were traditional border crossings, and we should still put in the systems to monitor people crossing those borders, to be able to first sell their goods, and second get their goods.

So it is very important data and how these data are being produced to respond locally to this disease. Thank you.

Senator SHAHEEN. Thank you all very much for being here today and for your great work.

Senator COONS. Thank you, Senator Shaheen. And thank you, Senator, for focusing us on what are some of the basic questions here. Having invested billions of dollars through PEPFAR in what is understood as the fight against HIV/AIDS, we have also strengthened health systems in dozens of countries. And the progress in fighting polio, for example, has largely been made possible by the health system investments made through PEPFAR. It is our hope that we will focus our response to Ebola in also strengthening systems regionally.

Senator Markey.

Senator MARKEY. Thank you, Mr. Chairman. Thank you for having this very important hearing.

Dr. Farmer, could you talk a little bit about the different cultures in Liberia as opposed to Sierra Leone and Guinea?

And we congratulate you, Madam President, for your tremendous leadership and work in helping to really focus in and isolate this problem in your country.

But just generally speaking, could you just explain why it is so successful in Liberia and not so much in the other two countries?

Dr. FARMER. Thank you, Senator.

He is setting me up, Madam President, because he knows I also have a Ph.D. in anthropology, which makes me cautious in answering.

I have heard, and read as well, about differences in those two countries that are fundamentally cultural, linguistic, historical differences that would determine the pace at which there has been uptake, for example, of safe burials or improved infection control practices. You have heard those claims made as well.

I am not sure that it is a good idea to put too much faith in those claims yet because we have failed so far in Sierra Leone to have a real collision between modern medicine, including prevention, and Ebola, and that is true as far as safe burials goes as well.

So, the focus for us, as Anne said, should be on listening to people, on talking to religious leaders, and that has been done perhaps more successfully in Liberia than elsewhere, and I wish I knew more about Guinea. But in each of these places, the response needs to do that better, to listen more carefully, to engage with religious leaders and families in their homes, and to have frontline workers be our other bridge, as well as religious communities, to the household.

It is not that that is an a-cultural process, right? But that is something that is—working with community health workers, in my experience, has worked in Haiti, in Boston, in Rwanda. It is a structural intervention that needs to be shaped to local cultural practice but can give a very big return, I think, regardless of which part of West Africa we are.

Senator MARKEY. Do you think it would be helpful if there was a larger U.S. presence in the other two countries given what has now happened in Liberia, that if we ramped up a larger U.S. presence in the other two countries, that it could make a big difference in telescoping the timeframe that it would take in order to successfully replicate what has happened in Liberia?

Dr. FARMER. You know, I would just say having a larger expatriot presence is a good thing if those expatriots, regardless of their origin, have the skills that are needed, and some of those skills are clinical skills, as was noted. That is, delivery is a big problem, Senator. We have the right ideas, we have the information, but we are not delivering, especially that last mile, in rural areas.

So logisticians we still lack. President Sirleaf said before that there is more electricity generated to power the Dallas Cowboys stadium than the entire country of Liberia.

So there are things that we need, and I would say bring it on. I think the United States, as Pape Gaye said, we have had this mantle of leadership in global health for the last dozen years, if not 15, and I think we would be welcome. So are the Cubans welcome because they are bringing delivery capacity, and so are those who can bring laboratory capacity and logistic capacity.

We have a long way to go, it seems to me, especially out in the rural areas.

Senator MARKEY. Dr. Peterson.

Dr. PETERSON. Thank you. I went from Liberia to Sierra Leone, so I got to see a little bit of the comparison, and when I look at the epidemiology of what happened, the Ebola epidemic made a round, a very fast, fierce round through Liberia, and we saw a lot more cases there early on than we saw in Sierra Leone. Sierra Leone is doing the same round, started in one part of the country and moving from hot spot to hot spot, but it has done it more slowly.

I think what we are seeing now is completely predictable because the place it had not yet reached was Freetown. It had not reached Freetown with its slums that have no running water, that have no sanitation, where people are very close together. It was just arriving there as I left a month ago. So Sierra Leone has a larger population.

In the end, are the epidemics going to be really different? I do not know. We can and should roll up a much stronger response in the urban and peri-urban areas, especially of Sierra Leone. It is possible in each of the countries they could do another round because it has been hot spot to hot spot. I think we are now ready to jump on and stop each one of those new satellites from expanding, and that should be our focus. So, back to the communities and identifying every patient.

Senator MARKEY. Thank you.

Senator COONS. Thank you, Senator Markey.

Senator Murphy.

Senator MURPHY. Thank you very much, Mr. Chairman, and thank you, Senator Flake, for convening this hearing.

Very impressive, Madam President, your testimony and your willingness to continue to be part of this hearing.

Senator Markey really asked the questions that I wanted to ask, and so I saw, Mr. Gaye, you nodding your head. So I am just going to extend the question to you, and I will really focus on the second half of Senator Markey's question, which is this query of where the United States should be and whether there is a role for us in Sierra Leone commensurate to the role that we have been playing in Liberia.

The British are there, but there have been criticisms of their ability to put together the kind of coordinated effort that we have helped, along with the President and her team, in Liberia. So, I would just love your thoughts on this question as well.

Mr. GAYE. Sure. Yes, I think there is a great role, a critical role, a strategic role for the United States to play. I am not sure that the answer would be to send more people from here. I think we should strive to foster local solutions. I think we should recruit President Sirleaf, who has taken great leadership here and who has really demonstrated what we need to hear more and see more from the African leadership: a high level commitment to the issue of the health workforce.

This is the human part of the health system. This is the entry point. Without the person, without the people, without the health workforce, we just cannot do anything. So we need to embrace this idea of a people-centered health system. When people think about health systems they usually think about infrastructure, the supply chain, or the costing. Economists come and give you a lot of the studies.

Paradoxically, we do not think about the most important element: the people we are trying to serve and the people who do the serving. This is why I think we need to, again, reelevate the importance of the health workforce, get the local commitment and look for local, national, and regional solutions in the long term. The United States is better placed than anybody to orchestrate that because of this leadership that we have been talking about.

Senator MURPHY. The quickest way that the United States can deploy more personnel is through the military. Have we reached the limit of what military personnel can do inside—we are talking about Liberia, but the British have people, other places—or is there a utility to increase the numbers throughout the region from the one sole source that we have that is quickly deployed, being our military?

Mr. GAYE. We need to win this fight quickly, so I think we need to bring all the forces we can to do that; as long as we also take the opportunity to reengage and recommit to really building the systems that are going to make sure this does not happen again.

Senator MURPHY. Dr. Peterson, I am going to ask a version of the same question that has been asked a number of times, which is how do we sustain this effort, and I want to just maybe ask you the question in this frame. We talked about the fact that there is a lot of money all at one time, and anyone else can answer this as well.

How do we think about time-releasing this money? Should we be thinking about mechanisms by which this money is spent over a longer period of time rather than all at once? If we think about how we actually make this be impactful 5 years from now, is this not just about what we choose to fund at the here-and-now moment? Should we consider reserving portions of it, or should we just spend it all now on the crisis and then come back to Congress and fight for more later on? As this might be our only bite at the apple, and if you have this kind of money and this kind of leverage, how do you spend it?

Dr. PETERSON. Thank you very much. I think perhaps both. We clearly have an urgent task that needs to be done now. But if we only address it from the urgent standpoint, if we do not reach out and deal with the economic issues, the drivers that are leading food insecurity and breaking quarantine, all these other issues are both important for the society itself and they are also part of the driver in the people's and the communities' response for infectious disease.

Our emergency response teams are not used to doing development. They are not used to working in community and talking in community. So I actually think we need a mix. We need OFDA in there saying, okay, what is the most important thing to do in the next 3 months, and we need the other side of the foreign aid that is looking at what are the systems, how do we build it, how do we build the capacity locally, and that will mean not one-year funding a bunch of times, which will always be urgent responses, but some longer term funding that says this rebuilding, as the President has said, is a long-term endeavor.

If I could also just speak to the DOD?

Senator MURPHY. Sure.

Dr. PETERSON. I think there is a role. I had a number of the faith organizations say please would we get DOD to help bring our stuff to us, home protection kits, PPEs, that they cannot get from one side of the country to the other side of the country. Our military is brilliant at that.

So there are roles, again, for our military, our aid organizations to work with communities and locals to get the most needed resources out to the places where it will make the most difference.

Senator MURPHY. This is a hearing happening in an amazing week in which this committee is grappling with a question of how we authorize force in the Middle East and whether there are ways in which we exert military influence and power that do us more harm than good. My hope is, especially with this new allocation of significant resources in the omnibus, that this is going to be maybe the pinnacle of success stories in terms of how the United States exerts influence around the world. This is a combination of humanitarian aid, public health dollars, and military support that can, at the end, be able to paint a way out of a crisis that a few months ago seemed to many in the short term to be unsolvable.

So as we all on this committee try to figure out what America's footprint moving forward in the world is, this is going to be a source of, I think, some very positive lessons learned.

Thank you, Mr. Chairman, for focusing us on this today.

Senator COONS. Thank you, Senator Murphy. And I would like to thank all the members of the subcommittee who have joined us today. Thank you, Senator Flake, for a strong and good working partnership through the course of this Congress.

I would like to thank all of the four folks who have provided testimony today, to Mr. Alvarez, to Mr. Gaye, to Dr. Peterson, to Dr. Farmer. Thank you for your service, for your example, and for your tireless dedication to improving public health. It is indeed our hope and our prayer that in our emergency response we are focused on building sustainably very strong public health systems in the three most directly affected countries and across the region, and that we will continue to work together in very real and meaningful partnership.

And to Madam President, thank you for being our very special guest today, thank you for providing remarks, and thank you for showing an unusual interest in what actually is done by Members of the U.S. Senate. It is not a common experience for us——

[Laughter.]

Senator COONS [continuing]. To have a President as interested in the deliberations of the Senate as you have been today. We are grateful for your tireless leadership of your nation, of the region, and of our world as we continue to try and find ways to stand up to the challenges of inequity and inequality, and as we try to believe a better future into being for the Republic of Liberia and the United States. Ours is a long and positive friendship between our nations, and I am grateful for your time with us today.

President SIRLEAF. Thank you.

Senator COONS. Thank you all very much.

We will hold the record open until the 11th for any members of the committee who might have questions for the four witnesses who testified today. Thank you.

With that, this meeting is adjourned.

[Whereupon, at 12:32 p.m., the hearing was adjourned.]

ADDITIONAL MATERIAL SUBMITTED FOR THE RECORD

PREPARED STATEMENT OF SENATOR ROBERT MENENDEZ

I'd like to thank Senator Coons for convening the subcommittee to examine efforts to halt the spread of Ebola in West Africa. I'd also like to thank our esteemed guest, President Ellen Johnson Sirleaf, for consenting to join us, as well as witnesses from the NGO community. I would also like to take a moment to not only thank, but to commend, the many brave volunteers who are and have been on the front lines on the battle to stop Ebola.

Madam President, our sympathies are with you and all the people of Liberia who have been affected by the outbreak. We stand resolute in our commitment to help end this very clear threat to international health.

We all know the figures associated with Ebola: over 17,000 people infected. More than 6,000 lives lost. What we must also keep in mind is the enormous toll this is taking on survivors and those in the broader community. Over 3,000 children have been orphaned. Livelihoods have been disrupted with a potentially devastating economic impact. Children have been out of school for months. Thousands of people are unable to obtain lifesaving interventions such as immunizations, prenatal care and malaria treatment because poor, already overtaxed medical systems cannot cope with the dual demands of crisis response and routine care.

The United States Government has led the way among donors, working with the Government of Liberia to halt the spread of Ebola before it becomes a pandemic, building treatment centers, sending thousands of units of personal protective equipment and laboratory materials to the subregion, and helping health officials with contact tracing, airport screening, training in safe burials, and medical testing and treatment. The U.N. has stepped up in an unprecedented way, with the establishment of the U.N. Mission for the Ebola Emergency Response. However reports from Sierra Leone about a rise in infections, and concerns about lack of accurate information about the widespread nature of the threat is troubling. We must work to ensure that we are sharing lessons learned from efforts in Liberia with our U.K. and French partners who have taken the lead in working with the governments of Sierra Leone and Guinea to bring infection rates under control. We can do more to share best practices on the health care response and social messaging efforts, and to coordinate our efforts on the ground.

While we may have seen progress in Liberia, the danger posed by Ebola is far from over. Congress is working now to act on President Obama's request for $2 billion in emergency funding for continued U.S. assistance to the beleaguered countries in West Africa. The money will be used to fund critical efforts by the U.S. Agency for International Development, the Centers for Disease Control and Prevention, and the U.S. military to contain and end the outbreak and to mitigate its secondary effects. Once the outbreak ends, we must look at ways to support improved global health systems in order to prevent another health crisis like Ebola from emerging.

Today I hope our guest and witnesses will address—among other things—whether and how we need to change the approach we are taking in the three most heavily impacted countries so that mitigation efforts are carried out in disease hot spots, and what we are doing to ensure non-Ebola patients can obtain care. I'd also like your views on what we need to do in the long-term to strengthen health care systems so that countries in the subregion—and beyond—to better respond to this type of crisis in the future.

Again, I offer many thanks to all of our panelists today. Welcome to the committee. We look forward to hearing from you.

––––––––

PREPARED STATEMENT OF SAVE THE CHILDREN

West Africa is now battling the deadliest Ebola outbreak the world has ever seen. The scale of the crisis is unprecedented in terms of geographic distribution, infection rate and the number of people killed by the disease. Save the Children is working urgently in Liberia, Sierra Leone, and Guinea to halt the epidemic before it spirals further out of control. Serious steps must be taken now to relieve the suffering of children and families affected by the outbreak. To this end, we urge policymakers to take the following actions:

1. *Fund the Administration's proposed Ebola emergency funding package.* In particular, we urge Congress to fund the International Disaster Assistance (IDA) account at a total of $3.5 billion for FY 2015 to make sure that as we address Ebola, we are not neglecting to fund critical responses to other crises such as those in Syria, Iraq, and South Sudan. This $3.5 billion includes:

- $1.4 billion requested by the administration for the International Disaster Account in the emergency Ebola funding package,
- $2.1 billion requested by the NGO community for the International Disaster Account for FY2015.

2. *Immediately strengthen public health systems in affected countries to address not only treatment of Ebola, but also the delivery of other essential health services.* One of the main causes of the Ebola outbreak getting out of control was weak, underfunded, and understaffed health services. It is therefore crucial to build strong local health systems to enable communities to prevent and respond to future outbreaks of Ebola and other infectious diseases.

3. *Invest in Education.* Children are losing out on critical months of learning as school year start-dates are delayed and schools in affected areas are closed. The postponement of primary exams and closed schools significantly increase the risk of permanent dropout and the loss of learning gains achieved in recent years by investments made by USAID in education. To ensure children receive a quality education, funding must be provided for quality home-learning programs, teacher training programs, home-based instructional materials, radio-programs, and text messaging that cover the national curricula.

4. *Meet the needs of vulnerable children.* Many children living in affected countries are traumatized by the loss of a parent or death of a family member and may be left without appropriate care. Stigma and fear may further contribute to isolation or rejection of children affected by Ebola. Efforts must be made to locate, identify, and register unaccompanied children to ensure that adequate alternative family-based care is provided. This care must be in line with the International Guidelines for the Alternative Care of Children. Moreover, children accompanying their family members to health facilities but who are not accepted into the health facility for treatment of Ebola should be cared for, monitored, provided with access to basic services and receive appropriate psychosocial support.

5. *Address the Impact of Ebola on household food security and livelihood activity.* In Liberia and Sierra Leone the price of food has increased in some markets since the start of the crisis, threatening to deepen the vulnerabilities of already poor and food insecure households. Some reports indicate that lower productivity also threatens the flows of production from the affected areas to main markets, with implications for wider food security in the West and Central Africa regions. The U.S. Government should invest in a thorough food security and livelihoods assessment in countries affected by Ebola to assess the impact that Ebola has had on income and food sources. In addition, targeted food assistance should be provided to isolation units, Ebola-affected families, and communities under quarantine and at risk of Ebola. Care should be taken that food assistance modality and distribution procedures align and support larger public efforts to prevent the spread of Ebola. Finally, trade must continue to and from affected countries to maintain economic activity and ensure adequate food and nonfood supplies.

We welcome the committee's attention to the Ebola crisis and appreciate U.S. Government efforts to address the threat of this crisis for the over 2.5 million children under the age of 5 living in areas affected by Ebola. As the needs in the region continue to escalate, so too must our humanitarian commitment. We sincerely appreciate your attention to these important issues, and look to both the administration and Congress to marshal the necessary support, including in appropriations legislation, to reduce the suffering and improve the outlook for the children and families of West Africa.

PREPARED STATEMENT OF CATHOLIC RELIEF SERVICES

Catholic Relief Services (CRS) is the official international humanitarian agency of the U.S. Conference of Catholic Bishops (USCCB), assisting poor and vulnerable people in 100 countries on five continents. Without regard to race, creed, or nationality, CRS programs address food security, agriculture, health, education, emergency relief, and peace-building.

As part of our integrated, multisectoral approach, CRS supports more than 180 health programs in nearly 50 countries across Africa, Asia, and Latin America. In partnership with the local Catholic Church and other faith-based and nongovernmental organizations, CRS health programs directly support more than 26 million people. These partnerships often connect us to communities inaccessible to government and provide the kind of local knowledge that builds sustainable solutions.

The West Africa Ebola outbreak is the largest since the virus was discovered in 1976. The first case was documented in Guinea in December 2013; since then, there have been more than 17,000 reported cases of Ebola virus disease (EVD), with just over 5,689 reported deaths in eight countries in Africa, the United States and Europe. The World Health Organization (WHO) has indicated that the outbreak may be stabilizing in some areas. Case incidence is stable in Guinea, stable or declining in Liberia, but may still be increasing in Sierra Leone.

Stopping Ebola transmission requires behavior change (people must understand what puts them at risk and take action to protect themselves), strong case management (prompt identification, isolation, and treatment of those who are infected), contact tracing (identification, isolation, and surveillance of those who have had contact with infected people) and safe and dignified handling of deceased bodies. Despite aggressive containment efforts, the World Health Organization (WHO) predicts that transmission will continue for at least 9 more months.

CRS has been active in the response since the outbreak began to spiral out of control, capitalizing on our existing programming capacity in the region and our extensive experience with natural and man-made disasters throughout the world. CRS has been working in West Africa for more than five decades (51 years in Sierra Leone, 24 years in Liberia, and 12 years in Guinea). In addition to committing more than $1.5 million in private resources, CRS has leveraged our health, food security, education, and other programs to rapidly and effectively respond to the Ebola outbreak. In addition, CRS has to date been awarded $5 million from the U.S. Government, through the generous support of USAID and CDC.

Though primarily a health emergency, the Ebola outbreak has wide ranging effects. It is setting back a full decade of development progress in fragile states emerging from civil conflict. The ripple effects of this crisis include the following:

• *Routine health care:* Prior to the crisis, the affected health systems suffered from inadequate personnel, low quality services, poor public confidence and poor health outcomes. Ebola is increasingly straining these already weak systems. Nearly 600 health care workers have been infected with Ebola, of whom 380 have died. Essential health services such as routine childhood immunization have ceased in many areas, and most health experts predict a surge in deaths from preventable illnesses such as measles, malaria, and diarrhea. Prenatal and obstetric care have also been compromised, and thousands of women are being forced to deliver at home without a skilled birth attendant, placing them and their babies at risk. In addition, Ebola survivors face stigma that can negatively affect their physical or psychosocial well-being. Many more people will die from lack of routine health care than will die from Ebola.

- *Livelihoods and food security:* Agricultural activities, including this year's harvest, will be heavily impacted. Many families have lost productive members and in some instances have been unable to access their farms due to travel restrictions and quarantines. There are indications that market disruptions and fears related to Ebola may result in price increases, limited produce in the market, and decreased income from cross-border trade with neighboring Mali and Senegal. Agricultural production is expected to be lower than usual, leading to an earlier and more pronounced lean season and negative coping strategies such as eating seed; FEWS NET predicts a "stressed" situation in heavily affected areas of Sierra Leone and Liberia.
- *Education:* Schools In Guinea, Liberia, and Sierra Leone have been closed since last summer, with potential far-reaching negative implications for children, who are losing valuable education time and may be at increased risk for child labor and early marriage. Universities and technical training institutions are also closed, which will make it difficult for countries to replace their skilled labor force (particularly health care workers).
- *Vulnerable children:* In Guinea, Liberia, and Sierra Leone, we are seeing a rise in street-children, in violence against girls and early marriage, pregnancies; hazardous under-age labor, and rising stress. We must be careful about hasty interventions that are not evidence-based and about "creeping orphanages" that devolve from interim care centers.

In response, CRS teams are setting up and supporting five community care centers to quickly triage and isolate possible Ebola patients. We are training 3,000 health workers and providing personal protection equipment in Guinea and Liberia to help provide access to routine health care for an estimated 3 million people. In addition, CRS was instrumental in the reopening of St. Joseph's Catholic hospital in Liberia's capital, Monrovia. The oldest hospital in Liberia, it serves as a referral facility for all other health facilities in the country, public and private. Now open, St. Joseph's is not only treating Ebola patients, but also offers routine health care, which has largely become unavailable due to stress on the local health system.

In addition, CRS is working to curb transmission of Ebola through programs that aim to educate and change behavior, with particular emphasis on using mass media, including radio and text messages, to promote awareness and increase knowledge. We have also capitalized on our strong connection to local communities, training religious leaders and volunteers to raise awareness and promote behavior change. CRS and our partners have already reached more than 2 million people with these messages.

The WHO estimates that 70 percent of Ebola transmission occurs through exposure to dead bodies. In Sierra Leone, CRS manages 19 burial teams (9 in Port Loko, 6 in Bombali, and 4 in Koinadugu) that conduct hundreds of safe and dignified burials in order to prevent further infections and respect families' religious practices. CRS is also collaborating with religious and traditional leaders to ensure access to and acceptance of safe and dignified burials.

Historically, outbreaks of EVD have been limited in scale and duration. The current outbreak is the largest and most complex in history, with more cases and deaths than all other outbreaks combined. Why has this particular outbreak evolved into a regional crisis? One reason is the location. In the past, Ebola has appeared in isolated, remote villages that had limited contact with outsiders; the virus was geographically contained until the outbreak quickly ran its course. In contrast, the current outbreak emerged for the first time at the intersection of three countries, spreading along porous borders and well-traveled roads until it arrived in the densely populated capital cities of Monrovia, Freetown, and Conakry where it claimed the majority of its victims.

Misconceptions, fear and distrust have also facilitated the spread of Ebola. Many sick people are not seeking care due to unfamiliar and sometimes frightening isolation procedures, low trust in health services, and perceived poor quality of care at treatment centers, helping to propagate the virus at an alarming rate. Traditional burial practices are another factor. Throughout the region, it is customary for relatives to wash and prepare bodies at home. While these practices are an important part of West African cultures, they expose family members to infectious bodily fluids.

And the slow international response allowed the outbreak to gain momentum while local authorities and NGOs struggled to respond.

But by far the largest contributor to the spread of Ebola has been weak health systems. Guinea, Liberia, and Sierra Leone all face a critical shortage of health workers, inadequate health financing, poor access to data for decision making, and weak supply chains. The virus appeared and spread for 3 months before health structures were able to identify its presence. None of the three countries had enough health professionals to trace the virus to its origins and isolate all those who had been infected. When tracing procedures identified infected people, many treatment centers quickly reached full capacity and many observation units were not fully staffed. Country health institutions also lacked the trained staff and volunteers needed to run education and awareness programs that would help people avoid infection and bury loved ones in a safe yet culturally acceptable manner. Those health centers that were up and running often lacked the necessary and life-saving equipment to treat Ebola patients and prevent the spread of infection. Personal protective equipment (PPE) is only effective if used properly but overworked health workers and improper training have resulted in nearly 600 health workers contracting the disease.

Furthermore, Guinea, Liberia and Sierra Leone are among 83 countries that do not meet the WHO's minimum recommended number of health care providers needed to provide basic health services (22.8 per 10,000 people). In most of these countries few, if any, local partners have the existing capacity in all areas (including clinical skills, strategic information, laboratory services, finance, health supply chain) that are required to sustain routine and emergency health services.

For this reason on September 23, 2014, the USCCB and CRS sent a letter to National Security Advisor Susan Rice to urge the U.S. Government to implement a multipronged approach: continue emergency response (case detection, treatment, contact tracing, safe burial) until the outbreak is contained, restore essential services (such as preventative and routine care) and focus on health systems strengthening to prevent future disease outbreaks from overwhelming local and regional health networks.

Strengthening health systems is critical to ensuring sustainability, equity, effectiveness and efficiency, all of which contribute to positive health outcomes. Building strong health systems will require expert technical assistance to all key stakeholders—including Ministries of Health, local technical organizations, civil society organizations and faith-based health networks—until regular monitoring demonstrates successful outcomes. An abrupt end to expert technical assistance will jeopardize programs and patients.

A successful effort will require a number of partners with varied expertise. The HIV epidemic has taught us that sustainable health care is multidimensional and all interested stakeholders must be engaged to bring their knowledge to the table. In particular, the role of civil society organizations (CSOs), especially faith-based organizations (FBOs), cannot be understated. Faith-based institutions are often the most trusted organizations. They play a vital role in the health systems located in resource limited settings. FBOs support national efforts; they offer complementary services, in many places assisting those the government does not reach; they help ensure accountability; and they advocate for strategies that match needs on the ground. As we assist countries in building resilient, high quality care delivery systems, we must ensure continued synergy between faith-based and civil society actors and local governments. The effectiveness of faith-based health system strengthening was demonstrated, in part, by CRS' AIDSRelief project. With support from PEPFAR, the 9-year program provided lifesaving HIV care and treatment services to more than 700,000 people through 276 health facilities in 10 countries. Working largely through rural and faith-based facilities, AIDSRelief established basic packages of care and treatment that exceeded what many thought possible in a resource-constrained environment. Instead of merely offering HIV tests and dispensing medicine, AIDSRelief helped our partners to build strong supply chains, operate high-quality pharmacies, manage state-of-the-art laboratories, and use timely-accurate data for decision making. More than 30,000 participants—doctors, nurses, pharmacists, and other health care workers—attended training sessions that built and strengthened their skills to provide high-quality medical, laboratory, pharmaceutical, and other services.

We urge the U.S. Government to lead other donor nations in developing and funding a coordinated, long-term humanitarian and development strategy for the affected region that rivals that of PEPFAR in its scale and scope. This new program for Africa should include immediate humanitarian assistance and health systems strengthening through ongoing technical support to build laboratory capacity, train and retain health workers, strengthen supply chains for medicines and commodities, and ensure sustainable financing for the future.

USCCB and CRS deeply appreciate U.S. leadership in West Africa, without which this crisis on top of so many other crises might have spun totally out of control. Our Nation's Ebola response will require a long-term strategy, sustained funding, and continued sacrifice from brave men and women willing to act out of love and concern for those less fortunate.

www.ingramcontent.com/pod-product-compliance
Lightning Source LLC
Chambersburg PA
CBHW080907290526
45795CB00007BA/2444